FOREIGN LANGUAGE COURSES

Welcome to the exciting adventure of Power-Glide Foreign Language Courses. We're thrilled to have you aboard and we are determined to help you succeed. As you go through the course, keep these two things in mind:

1. Keep it simple
2. Have fun

Most of us have studied language in traditional ways, where methods emphasized listening and lots of memorizing. Power-Glide's approach is very different. We offer a variety of activities all aimed at making natural learning possible.

So, rather than trying to master everything in a given lesson, find accomplishment in small successes and realize that learning a language is most effective when it's enjoyable.

One more note: Our mission is to revolutionize language learning. Everything in the course is aimed at helping students communicate in a new language. Here are some tips for you:

- Don't think you have to master everything in an exercise before you can move on. Or as we say, "Don't die on a page."
- Don't be afraid to make mistakes—learn as a child does!
- Feel free to jump around in the course.

If you wish to order additional materials or have any questions or comments for us, you may contact us by phone, fax, E-mail.

Contact Information
Phone: 800.596.0910
Fax: 801.343.3912
E-mail: info@power-glide.com
Web: www.power-glide.com
Support: support@power-glide.com

www.power-glide.com
Visit our resource-rich website packed full of sample lesson plans, cultural information, and lots of fun.

Let the adventure begin!

Product Registration

As a registered user, you are entitled to special announcements, customer support, and our quarterly newsletter. Power-Glide is committed to producing effective, fun, motivating language courses. To help us serve you better, please answer the questions below and mail in this card.

LANGUAGE PURCHASE
1. What language and type of course did you purchase?
 ❏ Spanish ❏ French ❏ German ❏ Russian ❏ Japanese ❏ Latin
 ❏ Complete Course ❏ Children's Course ❏ Bundle
2. Where and when did you purchase this course?
 ❏ Dealer Name _____
 ❏ Power-Glide ❏ Power-Glide Website Date _____
3. How did you become familiar with Power-Glide? (check all that apply)
 ❏ Friend ❏ Review ❏ Magazine ❏ Conference ❏ Card Deck
4. What most influenced your purchasing decision?
 ❏ Recommendations ❏ Reviews ❏ Ease-of-use ❏ Price
5. What other languages would you like to see us offer?
 ❏ Chinese ❏ Greek ❏ Hebrew ❏ Portuguese ❏ Italian
6. Have you registered at www.power-glide-school.com to take your tests online and receive credit for taking the course? ❏ Yes ❏ No

COMMENTS AND SUGGESTIONS
_____
_____

Name _____
Address _____
City _____ State ____ Zip ____
Phone _____
Email Address _____
Name(s) and Age(s) of Student(s) _____

COMPUTER CAPABILITY
1. Check the appropriate boxes.
 ❏ Mac ❏ PC ❏ Other _____
2. What is your current operating system _____
3. Processor speed _____ MHz, RAM _____ MB
4. Internet Access: ❏ none ❏ less than 56k ❏ 56k
 ❏ Other _____
5. Monitor Size ❏ 15" ❏ 17" ❏ 19" ❏ Other _____

NO POSTAGE
NECESSARY
IF MAILED
IN THE
UNITED STATES

BUSINESS REPLY MAIL
FIRST-CLASS MAIL   PERMIT NO. 286   PROVO UT

POSTAGE WILL BE PAID BY ADDRESSEE

POWER-GLIDE FOREIGN LANGUAGE COURSES
1682 W 820 N
PROVO UT 84601-9957

FOREIGN
LANGUAGE COURSES

Power-Glide
Children's Latin

Parent's Guide

by

Robert W. Blair

with

Dell Blair

This product would not have been possible without the assistance of many people. The help of those mentioned below was invaluable.

Editorial, Design and Production Staff

Instructional Design: Robert Blair, Ph.D., Dell Blair

Project Coordinator: James Blair

Development Manager: Erik D. Holley

Story Writer: Aaron Eastley

Cover Design: Guy Francis

Contributing Editors: Aaron Eastley, Erik D. Holley

Voices, Audiocassettes: Dell Blair, Julia Blair, Robert Blair, Aaron Eastley, Loren Higbee, Julia Young, Margaret Young

Illustrator: Apryl Robertson

Translators: Robert Blair, Loren Higbee

Music: SYNTH Sound Recording, Stock-Music.com

Audio Recording, Editing and Mixing: Benjamin Blair, Geoff Groberg

© 1999 Power-Glide. All rights reserved.
Printed in the United States of America
ISBN 1-58204-032-X
PN 3243-01 (11/99)

No part of this publication may be reproduced, stored in a retrieval system, or transmitted, in any form or by any means, electronic, mechanical, recording, or otherwise without the prior written permission of Power-Glide.

Power-Glide Foreign Language Courses
1682 W 820 N, Provo, UT 84601

Power-Glide **Children's Latin**

Contents

Introduction . . . . P-v

Adventure: In the Cavern of the Sea Turtles P-1

Adventure: Trapped on the Other Side of the Island! P-5

Familiar Phrases P-8

Adventure: Meeting Marcus on the Beach P-11

Match and Learn P-15

A Girl and a Mouse P-19

Adventure: Jungle Hike to the Village P-29

Lines and Figures P-31

Adventure: At the Village Market. P-39

Colors at the Market P-40

Adventure: Meeting Claudia at the Market P-49

Body Parts. P-52

Adventure: The Search for Aeneas P-65

A Boy and a Bear P-68

Adventure: To the Waterfall! P-77

A Hungry Giant P-80

Adventure: Cliff Climbing and Jungle Camp P-99

The Broken Window P-101

Adventure: Up and Up, to Antonia's P-123

The Key to the King's Kingdom. P-125

Adventure: Trek to the High Mountain Pass P-131

Aeneas' Challenge P-133

Adventure: Reunion with Old Friends P-149

A Note to Parents

Basic Course Objectives

The major goal of this course is to get children excited about communicating in another language. The adventure story, the variety of activities, and the simplified teaching methods employed in the course are all designed to make learning interesting and fun.

This course is primarily for children Kindergarten through 4th grade. Course activities are designed specifically with these learners in mind and include matching games, story telling, speaking, drawing, creative thinking, acting, and guessing—all things which children do for fun!

Ultimately, children who complete the course can expect to understand an impressive amount of Latin, including several common Latin phrases, some complete Latin sentences, Latin numbers, colors, and body part words, and instructions for drawing and acting given in Latin. They will also be able to understand stories told all or mostly in Latin, to retell these stories using Latin themselves, and to make up stories of their own using words and sentence patterns they have learned.

Children who complete the course will be well prepared to continue learning at a more advanced level, and they will have the foundation that will make learning at that level just as fun and interesting, albeit more challenging than in this course.

Teaching Techniques

This course allows your children to learn by doing: to learn through enjoyable experiences. The idea is to put the experience first and the explanation after. This is important to note because it is directly opposite to how teaching—and especially foreign language teaching—is traditionally done. Typically foreign language teachers spend the majority of their time explaining complex grammar and syntax rules, and drilling students on vocabulary. In this traditional mode, rules and lists come first and experience comes last. Learning experientially, on the other hand, simulates the natural language acquisition process of children.

When children learn their native languages apparently effortlessly in early childhood, it is not through the study of grammar rules and vocabulary lists. Rather, they learn the words for things around them simply by listening to others, and they intuitively grasp an amazing amount of grammar and syntax in the same way. By using activities that simulate natural language acquisition, it is not only possible, but normal for children to learn a new language quickly and to enjoy doing it!

Specifically, this course motivates your children to learn Latin by providing learning experiences in the form of matching games, story-telling exercises, drawing exercises, singing and acting, and other fun activities aimed at developing functional language comprehension and speaking ability. These activities contrast markedly with the exercises in more traditional courses, which tend to focus exclusively on learning some vocabulary, or on understanding very simple Latin sentences, without extending learning to the point of actually understanding and speaking the language. Significantly as well, the language your children will acquire through this course will be more useful to them than language learned through traditional approaches, because knowledge gained in fun rather than stressful ways is much easier for children to retain and much more natural for them to use themselves.

Using the Course

This course is carefully designed so that it can be used either by children working primarily on their own or by parents and children working closely together. Complete instructions, simple enough to be easily followed by children, are included on the tapes. However, to get the most out of the course, parents should use the thorough written instructions provided in the *Parent's Guide*. The *Parent's Guide* page or pages for each exercise state exercise objectives, provide instructions for students and teaching tips for parents, and give a full audio transcript. Using these helps, parents or other adults can enhance the course significantly by acting as facilitators: reviewing instructions, encouraging creativity and course participation, providing frequent opportunities for children to display what they have learned, rewarding effort and accomplishment, and providing enthusiasm. Keep in mind that much of the real learning takes place as you interact with your children during and after the course.

Using the resources provided in the *Activity Book* and *Parent's Guide*, an adult learning facilitator does not need to know Latin or how to teach it in order to be a great learning partner. In fact, one of the most enjoyable and effective ways to learn is together, as a team.

Parents or other adults who know Latin can, of course, supplement the materials in this course very effectively. A proficient bilingual facilitator could, for example: (1) help children learn additional vocabulary by putting several objects on the table and asking and answering questions about them, such as "What is this?" or "Where is the _____?", and so on; (2) create on-the-spot diglot-weave stories by reading illustrated children's books such as Silverstein's *Are You My Mother?*, putting key words (picturable nouns) into Latin, and asking questions about the story or its pictures partly or completely in Latin; (3) involve children in making and doing things (such as making a paper airplane or finding a hidden object), giving instructions all or partly in Latin.

Benefits of Second Language Acquisition

Learning a second language has many benefits. Besides the obvious value of being able to understand and communicate with others, research in the United States and Canada in the 1970s and '80s has shown that learning a second language gives children a distinct advantage in general school subject areas. Seeing linguistic and cultural contrasts as they acquire a second language, children gain insight not only into the new language and cultures, but into their own language and culture as well.

Furthermore, a considerable amount of research has shown that learning a second language in childhood helps children learn to read and write their native language. Latin is especially useful as an English vocabulary-building language, since many complex English words are derived from Latin roots. For example, the English word "puerile," meaning childish or child-like, comes from the very basic Latin word *puer*, meaning a young boy. Latin is also an excellent foundation language for anyone wishing to learn one or more of the "Romance" languages that grew out of it: languages such as Spanish, French, Italian and Portuguese.

Our Goal

Our goal at Power-Glide is to change the way the U.S. studies language. We want to help people really understand and be able to use foreign languages, not just study them. This *Children's Latin Course* effectively launches children into understanding and being able to use Latin. We hope you and your children will find delight in the adventure of learning another language.

Power-Glide **Children's Latin**

In the Cavern of the Sea Turtles

This section contains an audio transcript of the adventure story your children will hear on the tape.

Instructions for This Page

Have your children listen carefully as the adventure story is read on the tape. Also, encourage your children to take an active part in listening to the adventure story. Ask them to respond to things they hear and have them say out loud words said by the characters on the tape.

Younger children might enjoy coloring the picture as the adventure story is read. Older children may want to follow along with the written audio transcript provided in this *Parent's Guide*.

Audio Transcript

Narrator: Welcome to an exciting adventure, unlike anything you have experienced before. In this unforgettable adventure, you will need to listen closely so you know just what to do. When you hear this sound… you know that it's time to go on to the next page. When you hear this sound… you know it's time to stop the tape. We are excited to have you join Power-Glide on the ultimate foreign language adventure. Are you ready? OK! Let's get started!

Narrator 2: The Adventure Begins: In the Cavern of the Sea Turtles

Narrator: You are on a camping tour with two of your best friends from school, Jill and Henry. Your group is staying for a week on a tropical island. On your first day on the island you have to decide whether you want to spend your week by the seashore, or camping in the jungle. You, Jill and Henry decide to stay on the beach. The first place your group visits is a gigantic cave that the ocean has hollowed out of the rocky cliffs. The ocean washes right up into the cave, swirling around rocks and up and over ledges. In the water and on the rocks, big green sea turtles are swimming and playing. As you watch the turtles climb around on the rocks and dive into the water, you notice that one turtle has left the others and is crawling behind a rock outcropping just to your left. Your friend Jill says:

Jill: Hey guys! Look! There's a turtle right over there! It's on our side of the rope!

Narrator: And Henry chimes in:

Henry: Oh, yeah. I see it! Wow, none of the other turtles have come this close to us. Look, it's crawling behind that big rock!

Narrator: "Yeah!" you exclaim. "I wonder where it's going?"

Adventure: In the Cavern of the Sea Turtles

Continued from Children's Activity Book, page 1

Henry: Maybe it knows the way to a secret hiding place full of pirates' treasure! Let's follow it and find out!

Jill: Alright. But it's almost out of sight around the corner now. Let's hurry!

Narrator: The three of you rush to follow the disappearing turtle. It's still on your side of the rope, so you think it's safe.

Henry: Wow, look! There is a secret passage back here. It goes right down into the rock! It's just big enough to crawl through. Let's go.

Narrator: "But where did the turtle go?" you ask. "I can't see it anymore!"

Jill: Me neither. But look, you can see that it crawled this way--through the opening. We can follow the trail in the wet sand!

Henry: Good thinking, Jill!

Jill: Wait a minute. It's kinda dark in there. We might get lost!

Henry: That's alright, I have a really good flashlight in my backpack. Here.

Narrator: "Oh, yeah, I've got one too, I think." you say.

Jill: And so do I! Let's go!

Narrator: So you, Jill and Henry turn on your flashlights, crouch down to get through the opening to the secret passage-way, and start walking through it, following the trail the sea turtle has left in the wet sand at your feet.

Jill: Wow! Look, guys! There are lots of starfish on the walls and ceiling of this cave!

Henry: Yeah! I've never seen so many different colored ones before. Here's a purple one with long thin arms, and here's one that's pure white. Cool!

Narrator: The walls of the sea cave are very wet and the sand at your feet is damp too. If any of the three of you knew more about the sea, you would realize that this meant the cave is often completely underwater, and you are in great danger. But you don't realize this, and you keep on going.

Henry: Hey! I see sunlight ahead. I think the cave is coming out above ground!

Jill: And look here, someone has carved stairs right into the rock! They must lead to somewhere. Let's climb up and find out where!

Narrator: The three of you climb up the rough stone stairs, being careful not to slip and fall on the smooth green seaweed. As you get to the top of the stairs, you feel the sun strong and warm on your heads, and you can hear waves breaking nearby.

Jill: Wow! It's like our own private lagoon! We've come out on the other side of the high pointy hills we saw out of the window of the bus as we were driving here! Remember?

Henry: Yeah. I remember the bus driver talking with Ms. Brown. He said the hills were so steep and full of spiders and stuff that it was impossible to climb over them! The other side of the island was inescapable, he said.

Jill: No, it wasn't inescapable, it was inaccessible. People there still even speak Latin, he said.

Narrator: "Wow," you wonder out loud. "Do you guys think we really have gotten to the other side of the island, the inaccessible side?"

Henry: Who knows? But let's explore these tide pools before we go back anyway. No one will believe us that we got here. Maybe we can bring something back to prove it, one of those coconuts over there or something.

Jill: Yeah. That would prove we had found a beach, and not just crawled around in a cave. Wow, these tide pools have tons of ocean animals in them. Look guys!

Narrator: The three of you move from one tide pool to another, and you soon lose track of time. The water in the pools is so clear that you can see right to the bottom of even the deepest ones, and there are hundreds of

Continued from Children's Activity Book, page 1

multi-colored fish that come out from behind rocks and swim around in the pools if you hold still and watch. And there are also lots of starfish, like the ones you saw clinging to the walls of the tunnel, and seashells with crabs and other creatures in them, too. Finally you say, "Don't you think we should go back now?"

Henry: Oh, wow, yeah! We'd better go right now!

Jill: Yeah! I don't know about you guys, but I lost track of time. I'll bet we've been gone for a couple of hours now. The group is probably getting ready to go! We were supposed to have a picnic lunch outside the turtle cave, but even that will be over by now. Let's hurry back before they leave us!

Narrator: The three of you quickly work your way back over the rocks to the entrance to the passage-way. But when you get there, you get quite a shock!

Power-Glide **Children's Latin**

Trapped on the Other Side of the Island!

This section contains an audio transcript of the adventure story your children will hear on the tape.

Instructions for This Page

Have your children listen carefully as the adventure story is read on the tape. Also, encourage your children to take an active part in listening to the adventure story. Ask them to respond to things they hear and have them say out loud words said by the characters on the tape.

 Younger children might enjoy coloring the picture as the adventure story is read. Older children may want to follow along with the written audio transcript provided in this *Parent's Guide*.

Audio Transcript

Corresponding Page from Children's Activity Book

The Adventure Continues
Trapped on the Other Side of the Island!

Narrator 2: The Adventure Continues: Trapped on the Other Side of the Island!

Henry: Oh, no! Look! The tide has come in and the tunnel is full of water! It's spraying out of the opening like a whale's spout! Hey you guys, we're trapped here!

Jill: Trapped! But, how will we get back? We can't climb over those hills, and we can't go through the tunnel, so what can we do?

Henry: I don't know. Wait for low tide again, I guess. I think it goes in and out, so the water should be low again in a few hours. But we're still stuck here until then for sure.

Narrator: Dejected, and more than a little frightened, the three of you make your way over the rocks to the small sandy beach beyond. You sit down under an overhanging palm tree and take out some snacks from your backpacks. As you relax and eat you start to feel more confident and adventurous again. You turn to Jill and say, "I bet if we walk along this beach we'll find a village or something and we can ask the people for help. Someone has to know a way back to the other side of the island, even if this side is 'inaccessible.' After all, we got here didn't we?"

Henry: Yeah, that's true. But didn't the bus driver say people on this side of the island speak Latin?

Jill: Yeah. He said that hundreds of years ago a ship carrying settlers from all over Europe wrecked on the coral reefs that keep ships from approaching this side of the island. Those who survived couldn't communicate with each other in their native languages, but many of them could speak Latin, so it became the language of all the people here. And even though today people from other places can visit this side of the island by helicopter, and

Continued from Children's Activity Book, page 3

some of the people here can speak English as well as Latin, most people still just like to speak Latin.

Henry: I though Latin was really hard to learn. My uncle took it in high school and he hated it.

Narrator: "Yeah," you say. "I thought it was a dead language—that nobody spoke it anymore."

Jill: Well, that's not really true. I know a little bit of Latin, because I want to be a scientist someday. My dad is teaching me, and lots of the Latin words aren't hard to learn at all—like lots of our English names for animals and stuff come from Latin. Our word "leopard," for example, comes from the Latin word *leopardus*. And our word "crocodile" is like the Latin word *crocodilus*. A hippopotamus is still *hippopatamus* in Latin, and a snake is a *serpens* or a *serpentem*, which sounds like our English word "serpent." Those were some of my first words my dad taught me, because they are so easy to learn if you already know English.

Henry: Wow, Jill, I didn't know you knew Latin! That's pretty cool.

Jill: Well, I don't know it… yet. But I am learning.

Henry: Cool. But what does that have to do with being a scientist? Do scientists speak in Latin?

Jill: Well, not really to talk to each other usually, I think, but my dad says that scientists use Latin names for things in nature, like plants and animals and stuff, all the time.

Narrator: "Wow, that is really cool," you say. "But isn't it true like Henry said that it's really hard to learn Latin? I mean, besides those animal names you just said, I don't think I know any Latin words."

Jill: Well, have you heard of a *gladiator*?

Henry: Yeah, I have, I think. Gladiators were like sword fighters back in Rome, right? They fought in a big stadium called the coliseum. We learned about it in history class.

Jill: Right! And *coliseum* and *stadium* are Latin words, too! See, you guys do know some Latin already!

Henry: Wow, that's neat. What are some other words we might know?

Jill: Well, how about *alias*, and *insomnia*?

Narrator: "An alias is like a fake name, right?" you say.

Jill: Right. And *insomnia* means that you can't get to sleep at night. And we are all *homo sapiens*, too, and those words are from Latin! Even *rex* is a Latin word that means king.

Henry: So my friend's dog, Rex, is really named "King?"

Jill: Uh-ha. Cool, huh?

Henry: Yeah, it's cool to know what those words mean. So using those words, we could say to someone that we are *homo sapiens* who will probably have *insomnia* tonight because we're lost!

Jill: <laughing> I guess so.

Henry: Hmmm. OK. What else can you teach us?

Jill: Well, that's almost all the Latin I've learned so far. Oh, but I do know how to ask, "Do you speak English?" and "Do you speak Latin?" To ask if someone speaks English you say, *Loqueris anglice?*

Narrator: "What?" you say. "Say it again."

Jill: LOW KWERIS…

Henry: LOW KWERIS…

Jill: ON GLEE KAY.

Henry: ON GLEE KAY.

Narrator: *"Loqueris anglice"*, you say.

Adventure: Trapped on the Other Side of the Island! Trapped on the Other Side of the Island!

Continued from Children's Activity Book, page 3

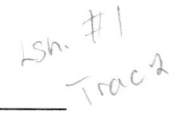

Jill: Good job you guys. Now to ask if someone speaks Latin you say, "*Loqueris latine?*"

Henry: *Loqueris latine?*

Jill: Right!

Henry: That's easy. Then how do we say, "I speak English"?

Jill: It's *Loquor anglice.*

Narrator: "*Loquor anglice,*" you repeat. "*Loquor anglice*... OK. So if someone here on this side of the island asks us, '*Loqueris latine?*' we can say back, '*Loquor anglice,*' right?"

Jill: Yeah. We could even say, *Non loquor Latine* first, if we wanted to.

Henry: *Non loquor latine?* Does that mean, "I don't speak Latin"?

Jill: Right on! *Non* means "not" or "no."

Henry: Cool! I get it!

Narrator: "Nice job, Henry," you say. "I guess Latin isn't as hard to figure out as I thought. Do you know how to count in Latin, Jill?"

Jill: Yes. I know how to count to five, at least. It's *unus, duo, tres, quattuor, quinque.*

Henry: Hmmm. Some of those sound kind of like Spanish. Let me see if I can say them. *Unus, duo, tres, quattuor, quinque.*

Jill: That's right, Henry! Now I'll ask you guys some number questions, and you see if you can answer them, alright?

Narrator: "Alright," you nod.

Jill: OK. How many of us are there?

Narrator: "*Tres,*" you respond.

Jill: Right! And how many fingers are on each of your hands?

Henry: *Quinque.*

Jill: Right! And how many suns are there in the sky?

Henry: *Unus!*

Jill: Right! And what if the sun and moon were both out at the same time, how many things would there be in the sky then?

Narrator: "*Duo,*" you reply.

Jill: Right on!

Narrator: "Thanks, Jill," you say. "But don't you guys think we'd better get going? If we don't find somebody to stay with by dark, we'll have to sleep on the beach!"

Jill: You're right. Let's get going. We can review the Latin you've learned as we walk.

Henry: OK, but which way should we go?

Jill: The only way, I guess: down the beach!

Narrator: So you all start walking down the beach, hoping to find someone to help you before it gets dark. It is still bright afternoon as you start walking, and the sun flashes gold and white off the smooth, warm sand, and the ocean glistens clear and blue at your side. You stay in the shade of the overhanging coconut trees as much as you can to keep cool. As you walk along you go over some of the Latin words and phrases you've learned so far.

Adventure: Trapped on the Other Side of the Island!   P–7   Trapped on the Other Side of the Island!

Power-Glide **Children's Latin**

Familiar Phrases

This activity lets your children see how many of the Latin words and phrases they can remember from the adventure story. The narrator will read through the words and phrases twice, reading the Latin and then pausing for your children to say the English equivalent before giving the translation. Reading through twice will allow your children to review any words they don't remember during the first read-through, and still be able to give the correct translation the second time.

Instructions for This Page

Have your children look at the Latin phrases in their activity books as they are read on the tape. During the pause after each Latin word or phrase is read, have your children say the English translation out loud.

If your children cannot remember some of the words, or give the wrong translation the first time through, simply let them listen to the correct answers given on the tape and try again during the second reading. If they still miss more than one or two on the second read-through, let them rewind the tape and complete the entire activity again, with your help.

Audio Transcript

Narrator 2: Activity: Familiar Phrases.

Narrator: Let's review the new words and phrases Jill taught you. As I say the words in Latin, try to say the right English words out loud. For example, if I were to say *quinque*, you would say "five" out loud. OK? Let's try a few.

Corresponding Page from Children's Activity Book

Familiar Phrases

1. *Loquor anglice.*   I speak English.
2. *Loqueris anglice?*   Do you speak English?
3. *Loqueris latine?*   Do you speak Latin?
4. *Loquor latine.*   I speak Latin.
5. *Non loquor latine.*   I don't speak Latin.
6. *Unus.*   One.
7. *Tres.*   Three.
8. *Quattuor.*   Four.
9. *Duo.*   Two.
10. *Quinque.*   Five.

4

1. *Loquor anglice.* <pause> Did you say, "I speak English"? Good!

2. *Loqueris anglice?* Did you say, "Do you speak English?" Very good.

3. *Loqueris latine?* <pause> It's, "Do you speak Latin?", right?

4. *Loquor latine.* <pause> You should have said, "I speak Latin."

5. *Non loquor latine.* <pause> Did you say, "I don't speak Latin"? Good!

6. *Unus.* <pause> Did you say, "One"? Good!

7. *Tres.* <pause> Did you say, "Three"? Good.

8. *Quattuor.* <pause> Did you say, "four"? Good.

9. *Duo.* <pause> Did you say, "two"? Good.

10. *Quinque.* <pause> Did you say, "five"? Well done.

Continued from Children's Activity Book, page 4

Were you able to say the correct English words? Good work! Let's go through the Latin words and phrases one more time.

1. *Loquor anglice.* <pause> Did you say, "I speak English"? Good!

2. *Loqueris anglice?* <pause> Did you say, "Do you speak English?" Very good.

3. *Loqueris latine?* <pause> It's, "Do you speak Latin?", isn't it?

4. *Loquor latine.* <pause> You should have said, "I speak Latin."

5. *Non loquor latine.* <pause> Did you say, "I don't speak Latin"? Good.

6. *Unus.* <pause> Did you say, "One"? Good.

7. *Tres.* <pause> Did you say, "Three"? Good.

8. *Quattuor.* <pause> Did you say, "four"? Good.

9. *Duo.* <pause> Did you say, "two"? Good.

10. *Quinque.* <pause> Did you say, "five"? Well done.

How did you do that time? Better? Great! Now, let's go on with the adventure.

Meeting Marcus on the Beach

This section contains an audio transcript of the adventure story your children will hear on the tape.

Instructions for This Page

Have your children listen carefully as the adventure story is read on the tape. Encourage your children to take an active part in listening to the adventure story. Ask them to respond to things they hear and have them say out loud words said by the characters on the tape.

 Younger children might enjoy coloring the picture as the adventure story is read. Older children may want to follow along with the written audio transcript provided in this *Parent's Guide*.

Audio Transcript

 Narrator 2: The Adventure Continues: Meeting Marcus on the Beach

Narrator: As you go over those Latin words and phrases, you make good progress walking along the beach, and finally in the distance you see what you've been hoping for all along, a house, or actually, a hut—a nice, big, comfortable looking hut. It's built right at the edge of the trees at the top of the beach, and there's a boy about your age playing with a turtle out in front of it. As you get closer, he sees you coming and stops playing.

Henry: Hey, look! Isn't that the turtle we followed through the tunnel?

Narrator: "Yeah," you say. "It looks like it to me, too." Just then, the boy waves and calls to you.

Marcus: *Salve!*

Jill: *Salve*... I think that means, "Hello."

Henry: Hello! *Salve!*

Marcus: *Loqueris latine?*

Narrator: "*Non*," you reply. "*Non loquor latine. Loquor anglice.*"

Marcus: Ah! You must be from the other side of the island!

Jill: We are. My name is Jill.

Henry: And I'm Henry, or you can call me Hal if you want.

Narrator: You introduce yourself as well, and then the boy tells you his name.

Marcus: I'm Marcus. It's nice to meet you. But how did you get here?

Jill: We followed a turtle through a tunnel, I think it was that turtle you're playing with.

Adventure: Meeting Marcus on the Beach   P–11   Meeting Marcus on the Beach

Continued from Children's Activity Book, page 5

Marcus: You went through the tunnel? That was brave. But you shouldn't have done it. It's really dangerous. You can only go through it at really low tides. And if you guess wrong, or a big wave comes in at the wrong time, you could drown!

Henry: Do you mean we can't get back that way, even at the next low tide?

Marcus: I don't think so. My parents have warned me never to go through it without one of them with me. It's only open at all every couple of weeks, and even then it's still dangerous.

Jill: Only every two weeks!? But our tour group leaves this island in one week! Isn't there any other way for us to get back? Can your parents help us?

Marcus: My parents are away, and won't be back for a couple of days. But maybe someone in the village could help you. I've heard my dad talk about another way to get to your side of the island, through a pass high up in the mountains at the center of the island. But I don't know how to get there. And besides, I promised to watch the house while my parents are away, so I couldn't go with you very far.

Jill: But could you at least show us how to get to the village?

Marcus: Well, yeah. I could do that. But from there you'll be on your own again.

Jill: This isn't sounding good. There just has to be some other way.

Marcus: I don't think so. That's why they call this side of the island inaccessible. It's really hard to get here. Boats can't make it through the big waves and the coral reefs, and the mountains down by the beach are too steep to climb. That's one reason why people here still speak Latin, my dad says—because hardly anybody has come here from other places for hundreds of years!

Henry: But you speak English, Marcus!

Marcus: Only because of my dad. He isn't really from here. He grew up on the side you came from, and only came through the tunnel when he was older. Then he met my mom here and got married, so he stayed. He still takes things over to the other side to sell sometimes, but mostly we just stay here. He has taught me English though, and there are actually quite a few people here who can speak English a little. The people on our side of the island love to learn everything they can. My dad has taught a lot of people English, and there are a some other people here who know French and German and Russian and stuff. Some people even know Japanese. Everybody tries to learn all they can.

Narrator: "Wow," you say. "It sounds like people here really like to learn other languages!"

Marcus: We do. After all, once you know another language, you can talk to people from other places. Even though we don't leave our island very often, we still have a really good library with lots of books our people have written over the years, and even copies of books the first people who came here brought with them. If you learn Latin, you can read some of our books!

Jill: I don't know how much time we'll have to learn. We need to get back to our group right away.

Marcus: But you may have an adventure doing that, whether you want to or not.

Henry: I want to have an adventure!

Narrator: "And I want to learn more Latin," you say. "Jill knows a little, and she was teaching it to us just before we got here. Some of the words were even like words we use in English already—especially the names of animals and stuff."

Marcus: That's great! Learning Latin is an adventure all by itself. And you're off to a good start, I'd say. My parents have always taught me that when you're learning something new, like a new language, to build on

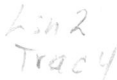

Continued from Children's Activity Book, page 5

what you already know. It sounds like that's what you are doing. Anyway, I'm glad you want to learn Latin. It's a treasure chest of a language, as my mom always says. Like just last week, for example, I was reading a book I got at the library that was all about the Trojan War and the founding of Rome.

Jill: Was it written in Latin?

Marcus: Of course. That's what they spoke and wrote in back then. The Latin we speak on the island today is a bit different, but I can still read the old Latin. It's called Classical Latin.

Henry: Did the book tell about how soldiers hid inside the Trojan horse?

Marcus: Of course.

Henry: Wow. That does sound cool. Just think, if we learned Latin, we could read things people wrote a thousand years ago!

Marcus: That's right, and even things from two thousand years ago. In our library we have lots of poems and stories and plays from back then that I love to read—we even have the Bible in Latin.

Narrator: "The Bible?" you ask. "Was the Bible written in Latin?"

Marcus: Well, it wasn't at the very first, but my mom says that lots of the Bibles that people read in other languages today were translated from the ancient Latin Bible.

Jill: So if we knew Latin, we could read the Bible in the same language the ancient Christians did?

Marcus: Yeah, and you would experience it a lot like they did. The words in the Latin version of the Bible we read as a family are really beautiful and powerful.

Henry: That's cool, Marcus.

Narrator: "Yeah," you agree. "It really is." You all sit silently for a few minutes, looking out at the sun setting beyond the waves. The bright yellow of the sun slowly darkens, and before it finally goes down the sun seems to get bigger than you've ever seen it before, and to light up the whole ocean in red and gold. When it is over and dusk starts to settle over the beach, Marcus says:

Marcus: Wow, I'm sorry! I haven't offered you anything for dinner! Are you hungry?

Narrator: "Well, we are a bit..." you admit.

Marcus: No problem. We have lots of food. Come inside and I'll light a fire and we can eat. We can drink the water from some green coconuts, too. And after we're done I'll teach you some Latin, if you'd like.

Jill: That sounds really good, Marcus. But don't you drink <u>milk</u> from coconuts?

Henry: Yeah. I've had coconut milk a couple of times back home, but not water.

Marcus: Well, you get water from young coconuts, from green ones that aren't all dry and brown and husky on the outside, like the ones you've probably seen. But when you first knock them down from the trees, coconuts are green with thick green husks. I'll show you how to chop off the husk with a cutlass or a machete and get to the water inside. Then when you're done drinking the water, we can cut the green coconuts open and scrape out the jelly inside. That's my favorite part.

Henry: Show us, Marcus!

Narrator: You all go inside the hut with Marcus, and he puts a generous meal out on a table for you, and uses a big machete to chop off the thick husk at the top of some green coconuts. Then with one last chop he opens a hole to the inside of each coconut and gives them to you to drink.

Marcus: Be careful not to let the water drip onto your clothes. It looks clear, but it makes purple stains that won't come out.

Henry: Thanks, Marcus. This food is really good, and this coconut water is too. It's cool to drink right out of the coconut.

Continued from Children's Activity Book, page 5

Marcus: I'm glad you like it. You can have as many as you want. I can climb our trees tomorrow and knock down lots more.

Narrator: "This is great food, Marcus," you say. "Will you teach us more Latin now?"

Marcus: Sure. I think I have a good idea for how to start, too. I'll teach you a few words in Latin, then I'll tell you a story that uses the words. How does that sound?

Henry: Cool!

Narrator: "Yeah," you agree. "It sounds fun!"

Power-Glide **Children's Latin**

Lsn. 2
Trac 5

Match and Learn

This activity is visual, audio, and kinesthetic. It is designed to help your children learn by listening and pointing.

This first exercise introduces the Match and Learn frames used frequently in this course.

Instructions for This Page

Have your children point to the picture of the rock as the tape directs.

💡 Younger children might enjoy coloring the pictures as the Latin words are said. Encourage your children to use these new words whenever possible. Make flashcards of the various pictures with the Latin words on the back and test your children regularly. Have your children create stories similar to the narrator's story at the end of the activity using these new vocabulary words.

Audio Transcript

🔊 Narrator 2: Activity: Match and Learn.

Narrator: Here are the things Marcus teaches you. First, as you already know, some Latin words sound a lot like English words. For example, some Latin names are a lot alike in Latin and English. Another example of a word that sounds almost the same in English and Latin is "flame." The English word "flame" sounds a lot like the Latin word *flamma*. Listen again, you can hear how close they are: flame...*flamma*.

Lots of other Latin words that don't sound quite so much like English words are still really easy to learn. For example, the Latin word for "woman" is *femina*. It sounds kind of like "feminine." *Femina*, feminine. *Femina* means "woman" in Latin.

One of the ways you can show that you understand words is by pointing to pictures when you hear words. Let's try it. Look at the picture boxes in your activity book and point to what you hear.

Femina... Of course, since the other box is empty, you point to the woman.

Match and Learn   P–15   Match and Learn

Match and Learn

This exercise builds on the previous one, continuing the introduction to Match and Learn picture frames.

Instructions for This Page

Have your children look at the pictures in the frames in their activity books and point to the appropriate objects as directed by the tape.

Audio Transcript

Narrator: There are two frames, or sets of boxes, on this page. The top frame has two boxes with the number 1 to the left of them. In frame 1 you have two choices. You have to choose between two pictures. Listen and point to the picture of the word you hear. Remember we're only looking at the two boxes in frame 1 right now.

In frame one, point to the *femina*. Did you point to the woman? Good! *Femina* is the Latin word for woman. And what is the other picture of? A man? That's right! The Latin word for man is *vir*. Say it out loud, *vir*. Good job.

Now look at the boxes in frame 2 and point to what you hear. *Saxum*. You know it's not the woman, the *femina*, so it must be the rock, right? Good job. The Latin word for "rock" is *saxum*.

Power-Glide **Children's Latin**

Match and Learn

This exercise builds on the previous one, continuing the introduction to Match and Learn picture frames.

Instructions for This Page

Have your children look at the pictures in the frame in their activity books and point to the appropriate objects as directed by the tape.

Audio Transcript

 Narrator: Here is another frame. Point to what you hear.

Vir... Did you choose the man? Good! But what is the other picture? A ball, a *pila*? That's right! It is a *pila*. In Latin a ball is called a *pila*.

Now even with only these few words I can tell you a short story in Latin. See if you can understand it.

Once upon a time a *femina* and a *vir* were walking down the street. They walked past a boy playing with a *pila*. Just then, the *pila* rolled behind a big *saxum*. The boy wasn't big enough to get his *pila* out from behind the big *saxum*, so the friendly *femina* picked up the *pila* from behind the *saxum* for him. The *femina* tossed the *pila* to the *vir*, and the *vir* gave the *pila* back to the boy. Then the *femina* and the *vir* walked away.

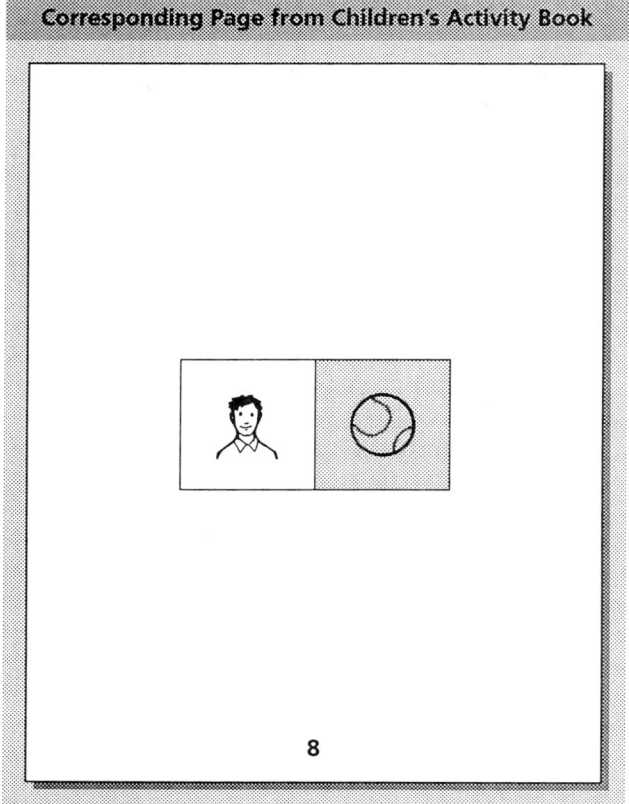

Corresponding Page from Children's Activity Book

Power-Glide **Children's Latin**

A Little Puzzle

This exercise uses a puzzle to help your children become more familiar with the vocabulary words they learned in the previous exercise.

Instructions for This Page

Have your children listen to the tape and point to the objects as the tape directs.

 Encourage your children to make sentences and comments much like the narrator does, using the Latin vocabulary in the puzzle.

Audio Transcript

 Narrator: Now that you're familiar with frames, let's try a little puzzle. Listen and point to the words you hear.

First, point to the *pila*. It is in the bottom gray box, right? Good! Now point to the *vir*. He's in the bottom white box, right? Yes. Now point to the *saxum*. The *saxum* is in the top gray box, right? Good work. Now point to the *puer*. The what? The *puer*. You don't know what a *puer* is? You know what a *saxum* is, right? And you know what *pila* is, right? And you know what a *vir* is, right? Well, there is only one other picture in the boxes. The boy? Yes, the *puer*. Point to the *puer*. He is in the top white box, right? Good.

That was easy. And now if I tell you my short story again, I can use the word *puer* for "boy."

Once upon a time a *femina* and a *vir* were walking down the street. They walked past a *puer* playing with a *pila*. Just then, the *pila* rolled behind a big *saxum*. The *puer* wasn't big enough to get his *pila* out from behind the big *saxum*, so the friendly *femina* picked

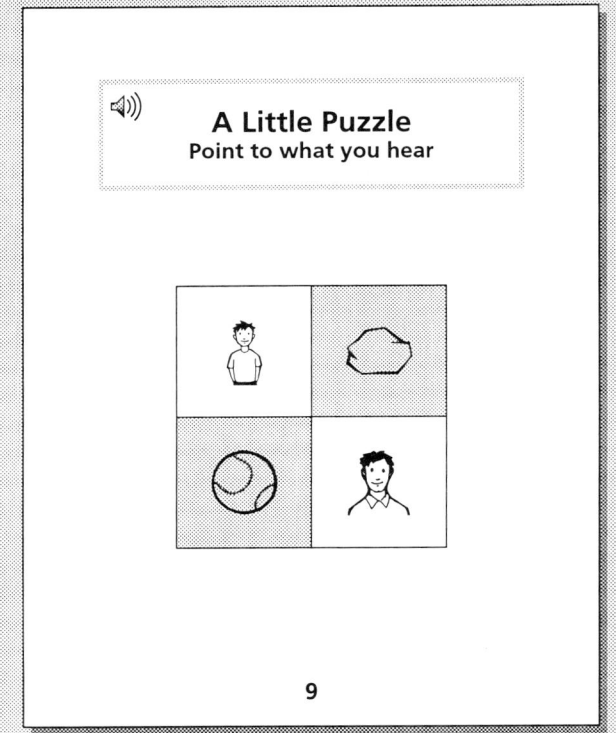

up the *pila* from behind the *saxum* for him. The *femina* tossed the *pila* to the *vir*, and the *vir* gave the *pila* to the *puer*. Then the *femina* and the *vir* walked away.

Did you understand everything? Good!

Match and Learn | P–18 | A Little Puzzle

A Girl and a Mouse

Although it is important for children to first understand spoken language, it is exciting when they begin to use it, and that is where the learning really takes off. In this and the following activities we continue with comprehension building, but as the activities progress, we gradually introduce conversation.

Your children will hear a simple story about a girl and a mouse several times. They will learn the character names and identify them with pictures. By the time we get to them telling the story, they will have learned to recognize the pictures well enough that they can tell the story simply by looking at them. This builds fluency because they not only go beyond simple comprehension to actual production, but they think in Latin as they tell the story.

You'll notice that the story is told with a minimum number of words, and in very short, incomplete sentences (Girl sees mouse. Mouse sees girl., etc.). We do this to simplify communication and pattern it after how children begin communicating in their first language. For example, children say "water" when they mean, "I'm thirsty, please give me water." The same idea holds true in this and other similar activities. We'll start with the most basic communication structure and build from there. Eventually, we'll teach language for more complete sentences.

Instructions for This Page

Have your children look at the illustration for the story "A Girl and a Mouse" and listen to the introduction to the story on the tape.

 Make sure your children understand each new Latin word introduced in the story. For those children who can read and write, teach them to spell each Latin word.

Corresponding Page from Children's Activity Book

Audio Transcript

 Narrator 2: Activity: A Girl and a Mouse.

Narrator: After teaching you those words, Marcus goes on to tell you a short story, a short *fabula*. This *fabula* is about a little girl, a *puella,* and a mouse, a *mus*. "Even though my *fabula* is very short," he tells you, "you can learn something about life from this *fabula*."

In this *fabula*, see if you can figure out why the *puella* in the story laughs, but the *mus* cries. The story is called "A Girl and a Mouse." In Latin it's called *"Puella et Mus."*

Match and Learn

This exercise is visual, audio, and kinesthetic. It is designed to help your children learn by listening and pointing.

Instructions for This Page

Have your children point to the correct boxes and pictures as directed by the tape. In the second part of the exercise, have them answer out loud the questions asked about the numbered pictures.

Audio Transcript

Narrator: Before he tells you his *fabula*, Marcus teaches you some new words to help you understand it. Look at the frame in your activity book with the white and gray boxes.

Point to the girl, the *puella*. The *puella* is in the top white box, right? Now point to the *mus*. The *mus* is in the bottom gray box, right? Now point to the cat, the *feles*. Is the *feles* in the top gray box? No, the *feles* is in the bottom white box, right? Now point to the boy, the *puer*. He is in the top gray box, right? Good.

Now, see if you can answer some questions about the words you just learned. Look at the picture with the number one next to it.

Number 1. Is this a *puella*? ... Yes, it is.

Number 2. Is this a *mus*? ... Yes, it is.

Number 3. Is this a *puella* or a *puer*? ... Did you say a *puer*? Yes, it is a boy, a *puer*.

Number 4. Is this a *mus* or a *feles*? This is a cat, a *feles*. Good.

Power-Glide **Children's Latin**

Match and Learn

This exercise introduces your children to some simple Latin grammar they will need to know in order for the story of "A Little Girl and a Mouse" to make sense in Latin.

Instructions for This Page

Have your children point to the frames as directed by the tape. They should begin to see how the Latin word endings are working.

Audio Transcript

 Narrator: Here are another couple of picture frames. Point to the box that shows the thing I say, OK? Don't worry if the words you have learned change a little bit, that's just how Latin works. Just listen, point, and learn.

First, point to the first frame, the one that shows a girl seeing a mouse. In Latin this is: *Puella* sees *murem*. A girl, *puella*, sees *murem*, a mouse. Or it could also be *Puella murem* sees. That still means "a girl sees a mouse."

Now point to the second box, the one that shows a mouse seeing a girl. In Latin this is: *Mus* sees *puellam*. *Mus*, a mouse, sees *puellam*, a girl. Or you could say *Mus puellam* sees. That also means "a mouse sees a girl."

So, let's practice. Point to what you hear.

Number 1. *Puella* sees *murem*. Did you choose box number 1? That's right!

Number 2. *Mus* sees *puellam*. It's box 2, right? Good.

Number 3. *Puella murem* sees. Did you choose box 1 again? Good!

Corresponding Page from Children's Activity Book

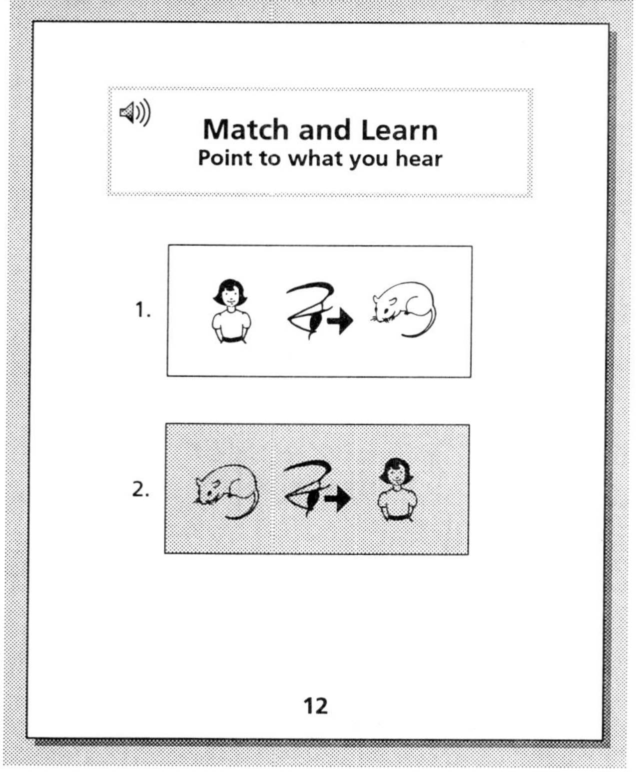

Match and Learn
Point to what you hear

Number 4. *Mus puellam* sees. Did you choose box 2? That's right.

Now I'll mix it up even more. See if you can still follow along.

Number 5. Sees *puellam mus*. Did you choose box 2? Right on.

Number 6. *Murem puella* sees. Did you choose box 1? Very good job.

A Girl and a Mouse · P–21 · Match and Learn

Power-Glide **Children's Latin**

Diglot Weave

This activity contains a simple bilingual or diglot-weave narrative built around two of the "characters" from the previous exercises: a girl and a mouse. This type of narrative was originally introduced by Professor Rudy Lentulay of Bryn Mawr University as a language-learning aid.

Instructions for This Page

Have your children listen carefully and follow the story in their workbooks as it is told on the tape.

 Have your children follow the words and pictures of the story with their finger, so that when the tape says the Latin word for "girl," for instance, their finger is pointing to the picture of the girl. This kinesthetic connection will enhance their mental connections between the Latin words and the ideas they represent. Once they feel comfortable with this diglot-weave, have your children come up with a diglot-weave of their own.

Audio Transcript

 Narrator: Now listen to Marcus' story about a *puella* and a *mus*. Follow along and look at the pictures.

Puella sees *murem*. *Mus* sees *puellam*. *Mus* makes sound "eek, eek!" *Puella* makes sound "eek, eek!" *Mus* runs, flees. *Puella* chases *murem*. *Mus*, however, escapes. *Puella* laughs.

Did you like that *fabula*? Did you understand all the words? I'll tell the story one more time and then ask you some questions about it.

Puella sees *murem*. *Mus* sees *puellam*. *Mus* makes sound "eek, eek!" *Puella* makes sound

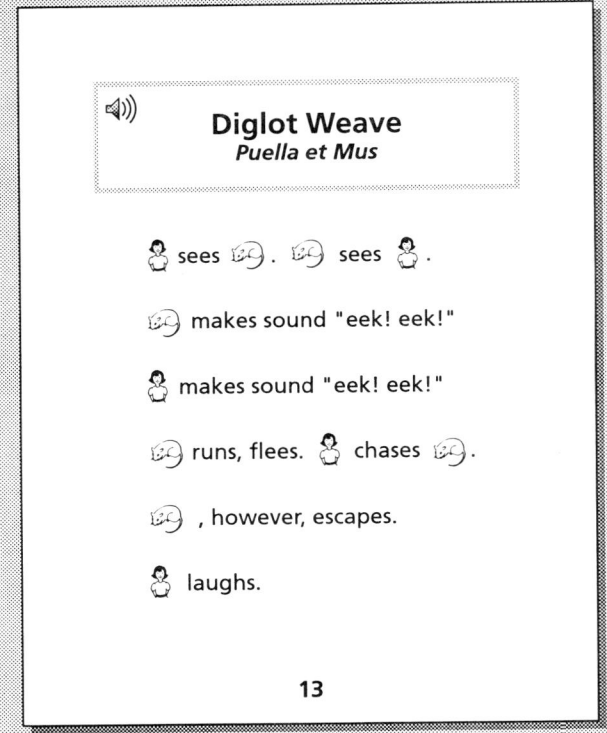

"eek, eek!" *Mus* runs, flees. *Puella* chases *murem*. *Mus*, however, escapes. *Puella* laughs.

Now, I'll ask you some questions. Say your answers out loud. Did the *puella* see a man, a *virem*? No. Did a *vir* see a *murem*? No! Did a *mus* see a *puellam*? Yes! Did the *mus* run? Yes. Did the *puella* chase the *murem*? Yes. Did the *mus* laugh? No. Did the *puella* cry? No!

A Girl and a Mouse — P-22 — Diglot Weave

Power-Glide **Children's Latin**

Match and Learn

This exercise uses frames to introduce new pictures in the story. This time there are two pictures in each box instead of one, thereby increasing the difficulty of the exercise.

Instructions for This Page

Have your children point to the correct pictures as the tape instructs.

 As these activities become progressively more challenging, the main objective is to help your children feel confident. They should not be overly concerned with correctness. Encourage them to point boldly as soon as they hear what to point to in the first half of the exercise, and to speak out loud in response to the questions in the second half. When your children guess wrong, let them know it's okay and to keep making their best guesses.

Audio Transcript

 Narrator: Before I tell this story again, I'll teach you some more words.

Look at frame 1. Point to the box with the girl and the running legs. Did you point to the top white box? Good. The running legs mean "runs," *currit*. Together, the pictures in this box mean "girl runs," *puella currit*. Now, point to the box with only the *puella*. The girl is in the bottom gray box, right? Now point to *mus currit*. "Mouse runs" is in the top gray box, isn't it? Now point to *puer currit*. Did you point to the bottom white box? Good.

Now look at frame 2. Now point to "mouse makes sound," *mus emittit sonum*. "Mouse makes sound" is in the top white box. Do you see the two pictures, the mouse and the "eek!"? These pictures together mean "mouse

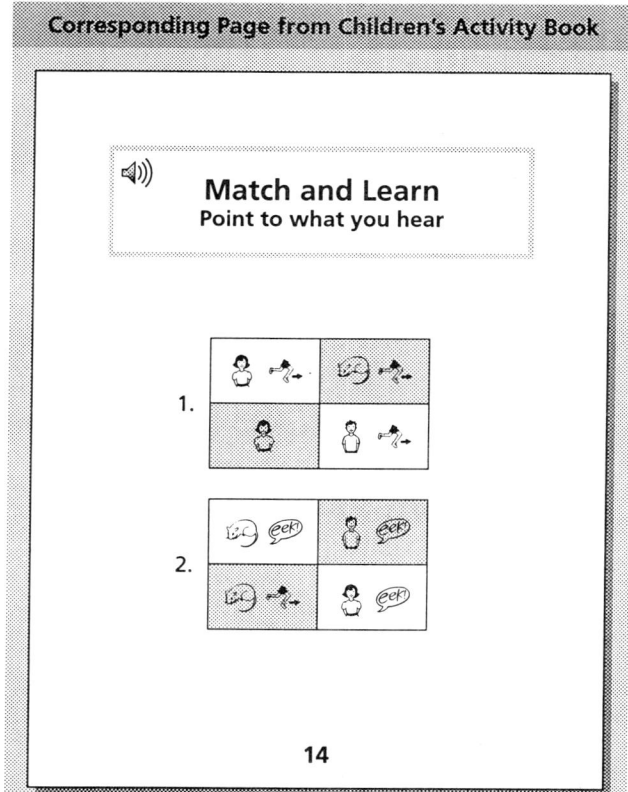

makes sound," *mus emittit sonum*. Now point to *puella emittit sonum*, "girl makes sound." "Girl makes sound" is in the bottom white box, right? Good. Now point to *mus currit*. It's in the bottom gray box, isn't it? Right.

A Girl and a Mouse — P–23 — Match and Learn

Power-Glide **Children's Latin**

Match and Learn

This exercise uses frames once again to introduce more new pictures that can be incorporated into the telling of the story. And once again, this exercise is slightly more challenging than the previous one because it contains some boxes with as many as three pictures to identify.

Instructions for This Page

Have your children point to the correct pictures as the tape instructs.

Audio Transcript

 Narrator: Now let's add a few more words.

Look at frame 3. Point to "girl sees mouse," *puella videt murem.* "Girl sees mouse" is in the top white box. See the three pictures: the girl, the eye, and the mouse? Together, the pictures in this box mean *puella*, girl, *videt*, sees, *murem*, mouse. *Puella videt murem.* Now, point to "mouse runs, flees" or *mus currit, fugit. Mus currit, fugit* is in the bottom gray box, right? Now point to *mus videt puellam.* Did you point to the top gray box? Good. Now, point to "girl chases mouse," or *puella persequitur murem. Puella persequitur murem* is in the bottom white box, right? Good.

Now, look at frame 4. Point to "mouse escapes," or *mus effugit.* The circle with the arrow pointing out of it means escapes—*effugit.* So, *mus effugit* is in the top white box, right? Now, point to "mouse makes sound," or *mus emittit sonum.* Did you point to the bottom white box? Good. Now point to "girl laughs," or *puella ridet. Puella ridet* is in the top gray box, right? Good.

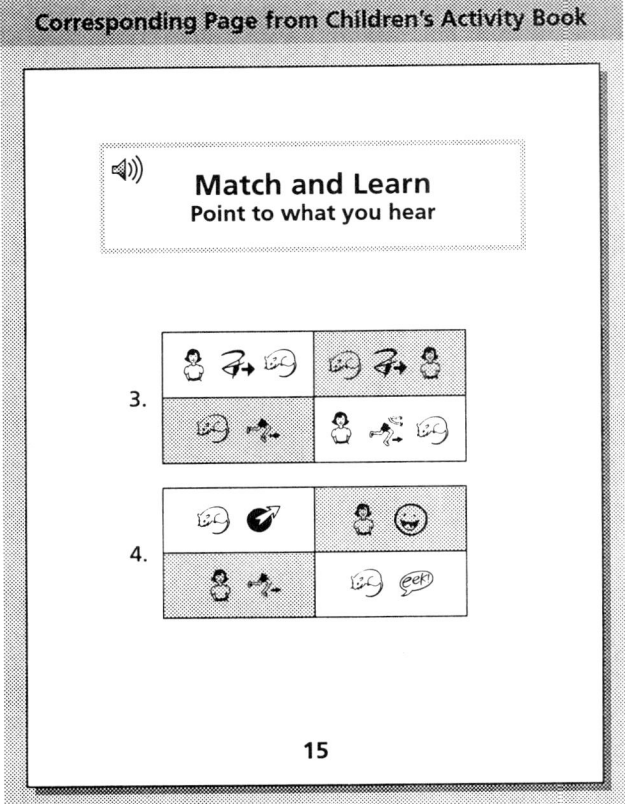

Corresponding Page from Children's Activity Book

Match and Learn
Point to what you hear

3.

4.

15

A Girl and a Mouse — P-24 — Match and Learn

Power-Glide **Children's Latin**

Rebus Story

This exercise is designed to help your children begin to think in Latin. This is accomplished by having pictures in their workbooks represent the Latin words read on the tape. This way your children will associate the Latin words with their English equivalents.

Instructions for This Page

Have your children follow the pictures with their finger as the Latin words for those pictures are read on the tape.

This is a good exercise for drawing pictures and creating flashcards. Encourage your children to create stories of their own!

Audio Transcript

Narrator: Now that you know the story, try to follow the pictures as I tell you the story all in Latin. There is one new word at the end: *autem*. See if you can figure out what it means. Are you ready? OK. Here we go.

Puella videt murem. Mus videt puellam. Mus emittit sonum: iic! Puella emittit sonum: iic! Mus currit, fugit. Puella persequitur murem. Mus, autem, effugit. Puella ridet.

Were you able to follow along? Good! And can you guess what *autem* means? You think it means "however"? That's right!

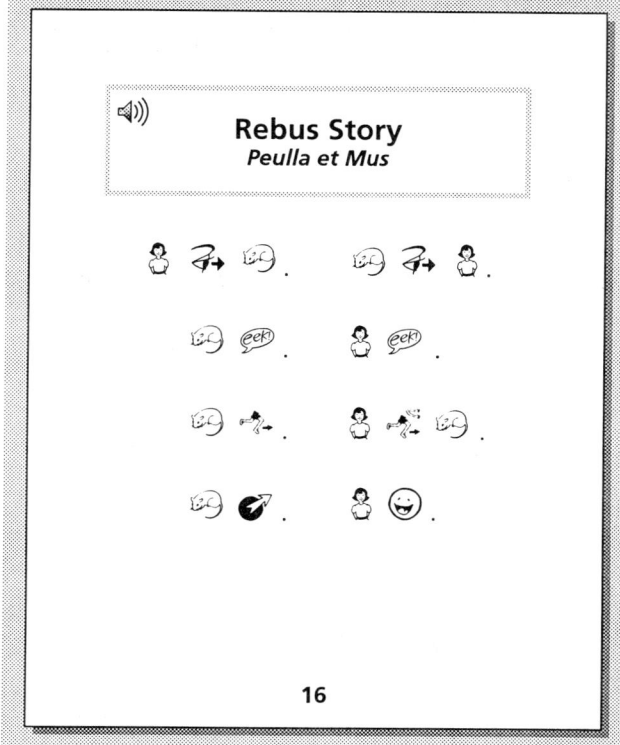

A Girl and a Mouse — P–25 — Rebus Story

Describe What You See

This exercise requires your children to use the Latin words they learned in the previous exercise to describe the pictures they see.

Instructions for This Page

Have your children say the Latin words for the pictures, or write them on the blank lines to the side of the pictures.

💡 Have your children say or write as many of the Latin words as they can on their own. Then you may go back through with them and help them remember those they missed. Continue to encourage them to guess when they need to, and to not feel bad when they cannot remember all the words or when they get one wrong.

Audio Transcript

🔊 Narrator: On this page are some of the pictures you have learned the words for. Say the Latin words for the pictures. Or if you like, write the Latin words for the pictures in the blanks.

Power-Glide **Children's Latin**

Story Telling

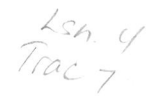

This exercise lets your children use the Latin words they have learned to tell the story of "A Girl and a Mouse" themselves.

Instructions for This Page

Have your children follow the trail of pictures (from top to bottom) with their finger, telling the story using the Latin words for the pictured items as they go.

If your children cannot remember a particular word, let them think for a moment, and then go ahead and help them. Your goal here is to encourage them to think as hard as they can on their own, while keeping them from getting frustrated or discouraged. Encourage them to create their own stories using the pictures in this exercise.

Audio Transcript

Narrator: On this page again, follow the trail of pictures from top to bottom with your finger, telling the story using the Latin words for the pictures.

A Girl and a Mouse — P–27 — Story Telling

Practice in Latin

The following exercise begins with the story of "A Girl and a Mouse" read entirely in Latin.

This exercise then asks your children to tell the story entirely in Latin on their own, using the pictures in the circle below the Latin text as memory prompts.

Instructions for This Page

First have your children follow the Latin text in their workbooks as it is read on the tape.

Then have them cover the Latin text, look at the pictures in the circle below the text, and try to tell the story in Latin on their own. Record how long it takes them to tell the complete story in Latin their first time, and then record their best subsequent time.

Let your children try telling the story as many as six or eight times, perhaps even looking back at the Latin text on the top of the page and learning the Latin articles and other connecting words found there. Have them rearrange the sentences, thereby creating their own story.

Audio Transcript

Narrator: Last of all, here is the story written out, all in Latin. Listen carefully.

Puella videt murem. Mus videt puellam. Mus emittit sonum: iic! Puella emittit sonum: iic! Mus currit, fugit. Puella persequitur murem. Mus, autem, effugit. Puella ridet.

Were you able to follow along and understand? Good! Now try to tell the story in Latin on your own, using as many Latin words as you can remember. Point to the pictures as you tell the story. Write down how long it takes you to tell the story in Latin your first time, then tell the story again, and then again, and write your best time after that!

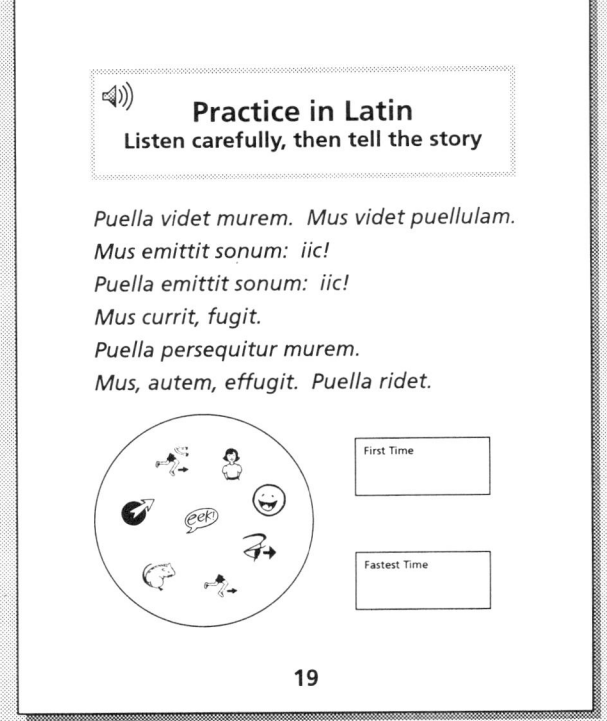

A Girl and a Mouse — P–28 — Practice in Latin

Power-Glide **Children's Latin**

Jungle Hike to the Village

This section contains an audio transcript of the adventure story your children will hear on the tape.

Instructions for This Page

Have your children listen carefully as the adventure story is read on the tape. Encourage your children to take an active part in listening to the adventure story. Ask them to respond to things they hear and have them say out loud words said by the characters on the tape.

💡 Younger children might enjoy coloring the picture as the adventure story is read. Older children may want to follow along with the written audio transcript provided in this *Parent's Guide*.

Audio Transcript

🔊 Narrator 2: The Adventure Continues: Jungle Hike to the Village

Narrator: After Marcus finishes his story, you all thank him for telling it to you, and then Henry yawns loudly.

Henry: <yawning> Wow. I'm tired.

Jill: Me too.

Marcus: Well, let's all go to sleep. That way we can make an early start for the village first thing in the morning. Here, I'll hang up the extra hammocks for you guys.

Henry: We get to sleep in hammocks?

Marcus: Of course!

Henry: Cool!

Corresponding Page from Children's Activity Book

🔊 **The Adventure Continues**
Jungle Hike to the Village

21

Narrator: Soon you are all fast asleep in your hammocks, swaying gently back and forth in the cool ocean breezes that blow through the hut. Before you know it, it starts to get light outside, and you wake up to the sound of Marcus humming to himself as he puts mangoes, papayas, bananas and other fruits out for your breakfast. "What's that song you're singing, Marcus?" you ask.

Marcus: What? Oh, you're awake! Great! I was just humming a song my mother sings when I sleep in late.

In English it goes:

<<<Tune: Are you sleeping?>>>

> Brother John, Brother John
> Are you asleep? Are you asleep?
> It is noon already,
> It is noon already,
> Get up now,
> Get up now.

Adventure: Jungle Hike to the Village   P–29   Jungle Hike to the Village

Continued from Children's Activity Book, page 21

And in Latin it is:

Frater Ioannis, Frater Ioannis,
Dormis tu? Dormis tu?
Iam est meridies,
Iam est meridies,
Surge jam,
Surge jam.

Jill: That's a fun song for waking people up!

Marcus: Yeah. And it works well, too! You guys are all up now!

Henry: Right on! Wow, what have you got there? It looks delicious. I'm starving.

Narrator: You eat all you want and then wash the sticky mango juice off your faces and hands. Once you've cleaned up, you quickly get ready to hike through the jungle to the village. You set off to the sound of jungle birds chirping in the trees and other strange creatures calling to each other in voices you've never heard before. Rays of bright morning sunlight shine through the leafy canopy high above your heads, and giant ferns grow all around you. Vines as thick as your arms hang down from the branches. The path twists and turns through the trunks of trees that look very old. Some plants growing near the path have leaves as long as you are tall, and bright colored flowers three feet across.

Henry: This is an awesome jungle. These flowers are huge, and look at that butterfly!

Jill: I see it! It's huge, too. It seems like everything here gets bigger than back home.

Marcus: I think that's true. All the sun and the rain make things grow really fast, and get big. With all the plants growing so close to the path, it can be easy to get lost if you're not familiar with the island, or if you don't have a good map. See, here's a map my dad made for me when I was first big enough to go into the village by myself. Let's stop and rest for a bit, and I'll show you where we are on the map, and teach you the Latin words for things on maps like dots, lines and shapes.

Henry: Alright. I love maps. Back home I used to look at them for hours, and wonder what the places really looked like.

Marcus: I like to do that too. And I like to go exploring.

Jill: Yeah, me too. Wow, this is a good map. Your dad must be a good artist.

Marcus: He is. See, right now we're here, between these two hills, and the village is over this way, about another two hours walking.

Power-Glide **Children's Latin**

Lines and Figures

The following activity is a learning game that uses pictures to help your children learn some new words. The activity is deliberately simple in order to help your children develop confidence in their ability to comprehend a foreign language.

Instructions for This Page

Have your children look at the pictures in their activity books and point to the shapes as they hear the words for those shapes read on the tape. The narrator will read each word twice in Latin, then go back through the words in Latin one by one, and finally read the Latin words all together.

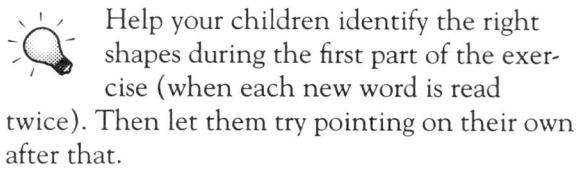

Help your children identify the right shapes during the first part of the exercise (when each new word is read twice). Then let them try pointing on their own after that.

Have your children pause the tape as needed to have time to give their answers.

Audio Transcript

Narrator 2: Activity: Lines and Figures.

Narrator: Here on your activity book page are the figures Marcus teaches you. The first thing on your page is a single line, *una linea.* Can you guess what two lines would be? That's right! *Duae lineae!* The other things are figures, *figurae.* Besides the line there are *tres figurae.* There is *unum triangulum,* a triangle, *unum quadratum,* a square, and *unus circulus,* a circle.

Now point to what you hear. *Unus circulus. Unum quadratum. Unum triangulum. Una linea.* Did you point to them all? Good job!

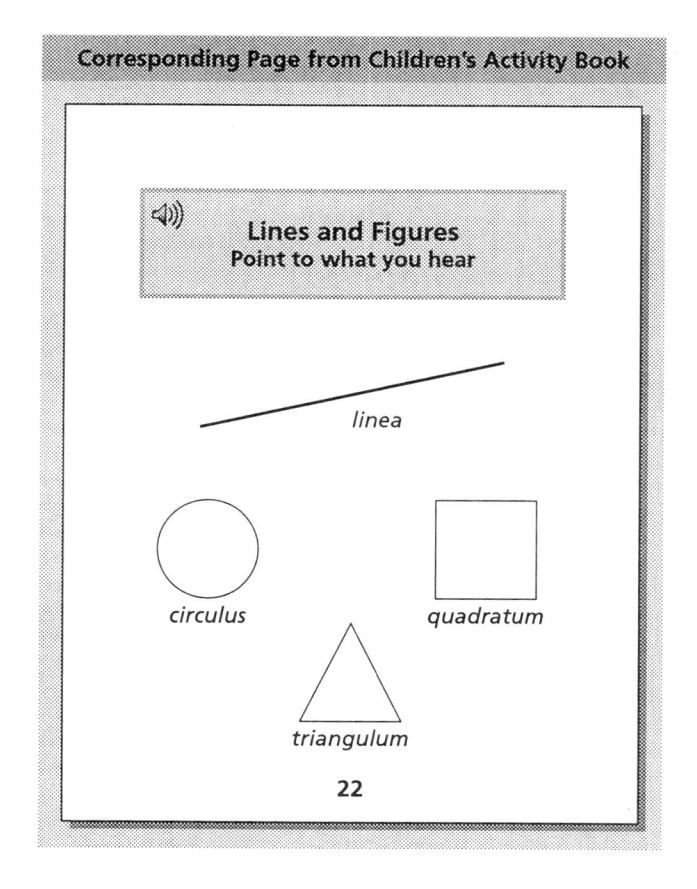

Corresponding Page from Children's Activity Book

Lines and Figures
Point to what you hear

linea

circulus *quadratum*

triangulum

22

Lines and Figures   P–31   Lines and Figures

Look and Listen

This exercise uses the shapes from the previous page in several different combinations.

Learning to identify more than one of the same shape (two circles or three lines, for instance) and various shapes grouped together will give your children added confidence.

Instructions for This Page

Have your children look at the numbered pictures of shapes and sets of shapes in their activity books as the words for those shapes are read on the tape.

Encourage your children to point to each shape with their finger and count when appropriate as the words are read on the tape. For example, on number 12 they could point to the two squares one by one immediately after *"duo quadrata"* is read on the tape, then point to the line as "and *una linea*" is read on the tape.

Audio Transcript

Narrator: On this page, point to what you hear.

Number 1. *Circulus*...circle. *Unus circulus.*

Number 2. *Quadratum*...square. *Unum quadratum.*

Number 3. *Triangulum*...triangle. *Unum triangulum.*

Number 4. *Linea*...line. *Una linea.*

Number 5. *Unum triangulum et unum quadratum.* One triangle and one square.

Number 6. *Unus circulus et unum triangulum.* One circle and one triangle.

Number 7. *Duo circuli.* Two circles.

Number 8. *Tres circuli et duo triangula.* Three circles and two triangles.

Number 9. *Duo quadrata et tres lineae.* Two squares and three lines.

Number 10. *Duo circuli et unum triangulum.* Two circles and one triangle.

Number 11. *Tres lineae et unus circulus.* Three lines and one circle.

Number 12. *Duo quadrata et una linea.* Two squares and one line.

Well done.

Power-Glide **Children's Latin**

Point to What You Hear

This time the shapes will be read in Latin only. This exercise builds the same identification skills as the previous exercise, and also reviews the basic Latin numbers.

Instructions for This Page

As before, have your children look at the pictures in their activity books and point to the shapes and sets of shapes as they hear the Latin numbers and words for those shapes read on the tape. Then encourage them to call out the Latin words before they are read on the tape.

Audio Transcript

Narrator: Now look and listen again. This time I'll say just the Latin names of the shapes, and I'll mix up the order. You point to the shapes that you hear. Ready? OK.

Point to *duo circuli*. It's number 7, right?

Now point to *unum triangulum*. It's number 3, right?

Now point to *duo quadrata et una linea*. It's number 12, right?

Now point to *duo quadrata et tres lineae*. It's number 9, right?

Now point to *una linea*. It's number 4, right?

Now point to *unus circulus*. It's number 1, right?

Now point to *unum triangulum et unum quadratum*. It's number 5, right?

Now point to *tres lineae et unus circulus*. It's number 11, right?

Corresponding Page from Children's Activity Book

Point to What You Hear

1. ◯
2. ▢
3. △
4. ╱
5. △▢
6. ◯△
7. ◯◯
8. ◯◯◯△△
9. ▢▢///
10. ◯◯△
11. ///◯
12. ▢▢╱

24

Now point to *unum quadratum*. It's number 2, right?

Now point to *tres circuli et duo triangula*. It's number 8, right?

Now point to *unus circulus et unum triangulum*. It's number 6, right?

And last of all, point to *duo circuli et unum triangulum*. It's number 10, isn't it?

Were you able to point to most of them? Very well done.

Lines and Figures

Match and Learn

This exercise is visual, audio, and kinesthetic. It is designed to help your children learn by listening and pointing.

Instructions for This Page

Have your children look at the pictures in each numbered frame in their activity books and point to the box which contains the shapes whose names are read on the tape. The names for the shapes in three of the four boxes will be read before the tape goes on to the next frame. This will allow for a process of elimination to take place as your children go through the boxes in each numbered frame.

If it's helpful or fun, encourage your children to mark off the boxes already selected as they go along.

Audio Transcript

Narrator: Now let's do some match and learn activities. Point to what you hear.

Look at frame 1. Point to *unus circulus.* It's in the bottom white box, right? Good. Now point to *duo triangula.* It's in the top white box, right? Now point to *unum triangulum.* It's the bottom gray box. Now point to *duo circuli.* It's the top gray box.

Look at frame 2. Point to the box with *duo circuli.* It's the top gray box, right? Now point to *duo triangula.* It's the bottom gray box. Now point to *duae lineae.* It's the top white box.

Now look at frame 3. Point to the *quadratum.* It's the top white box, right? Now point to *duo quadrata.* It's the top gray box. Now point

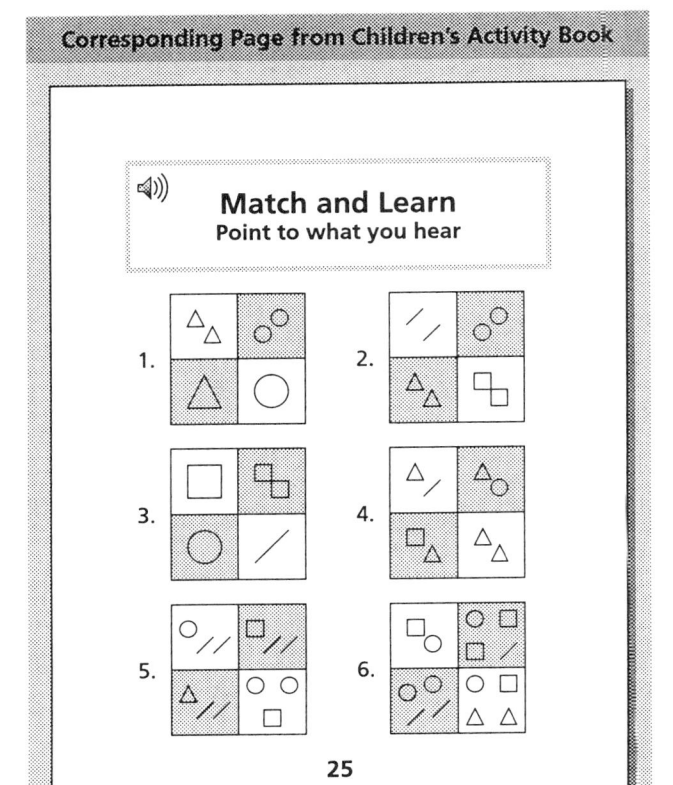

to *una linea.* It's the bottom white box, right? Well done!

Now look at frame 4. Point to *duo triangula.* It's the bottom white box, right? Now point to *unum quadratum et unum triangulum.* It's the bottom gray box. Now point to *unum triangulum et una linea.* It's the top white box, right?

Now look at frame 5. Point to *duae lineae et unum triangulum.* It's the bottom gray box. Now point to *duo circuli et unum quadratum.* It's the bottom white box. Now point to *duae lineae et unum quadratum.* It's the top gray box.

Now look at frame 6. Point to *unus circulus, duo triangula et unum quadratum.* It's the bottom white box, isn't it? Now point to *unus circulus, duo quadrata et una linea.* It's the top gray box. Now point to *unum quadratum et unus circulus.* It's the top white box, right?

Lines and Figures

Listen and Draw

After your children develop their ability to comprehend, they'll begin to produce. This exercise reinforces their ability to comprehend by having your children do something kinesthetic and creative: drawing what is heard. Drawing helps your children internalize what is being learned because they will have to interpret what is heard in a creative form.

Instructions for This Page

Have your children listen to the descriptions of sets of shapes read on the tape and draw what they hear. These will be combinations of multiple numbers of the same shapes and various other shapes (for instance, number 1 calls for "Two lines and one circle"). Have your children draw all of the shapes for each number in the gray "chalkboard" box next to that number.

Have your children pause the tape as needed to have time to give their answers.

Audio Transcript

Narrator: These chalkboards are for you to draw on. You'll be drawing squares, *quadrata*; circles, *circuli*; triangles, *triangula*; and lines, *lineae*.

I'll name the shapes and you draw them. You can turn off the tape while you get something to write with if you need to. Are you ready? OK. Here we go.

Number 1. *Duae lineae et unus circulus. Duae lineae et unus circulus.* Two lines and one circle.

Number 2. *Duo circuli et una linea. Duo circuli et una linea.* Two circles and one line.

Corresponding Page from Children's Activity Book

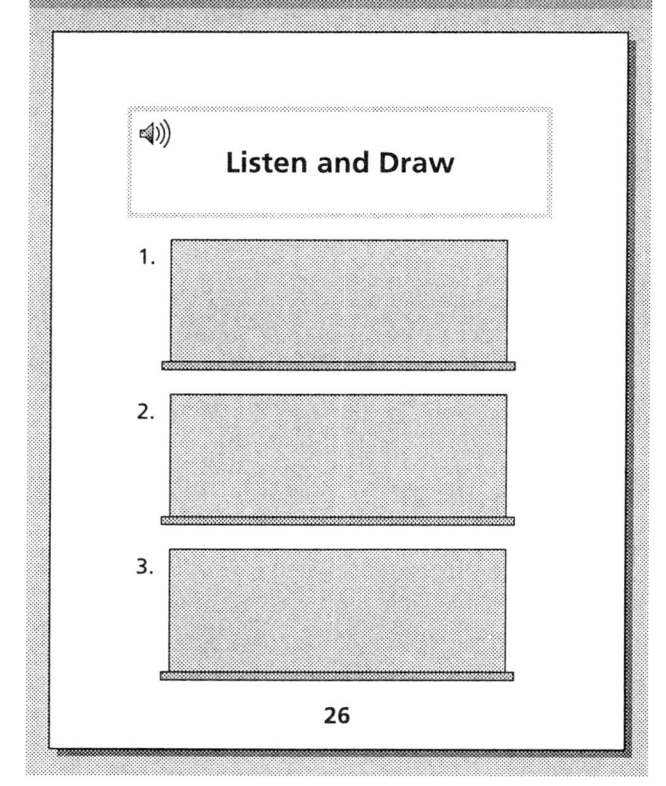

Listen and Draw

1.

2.

3.

26

Number 3. *Una linea, unum quadratum, unus circulus, et unum triangulum. Una linea, unum quadratum, unus circulus, et unum triangulum.* One line, one square, one circle, and one triangle.

Listen and Draw

Here are the chalkboards with the correct shapes drawn on them.

Instructions for This Page

Compare these drawings to those of your children. Point out the similarities and the differences. Be sure to compliment your children on what they drew correctly.

After reviewing your children's drawings, have them look at the sample "answer" drawings in their activity books as the corresponding Latin words are read again on the tape.

Audio Transcript

Narrator: Here are the same chalkboards, but with my drawings on them. Do your drawings look something like mine? Let's look at each chalkboard together.

Number 1. *Duae lineae et unus circulus.*

Number 2. *Duo circuli et una linea.*

Number 3. *Una linea, unum quadratum, unus circulus, et unum triangulum.* This is a full chalkboard, isn't it?

Corresponding Page from Children's Activity Book

1. *Duae lineae et unus circulus.*
2. *Duo circuli et una linea.*
3. *Una linea, unum quadratum, unus circulus, et unum triangulum.*

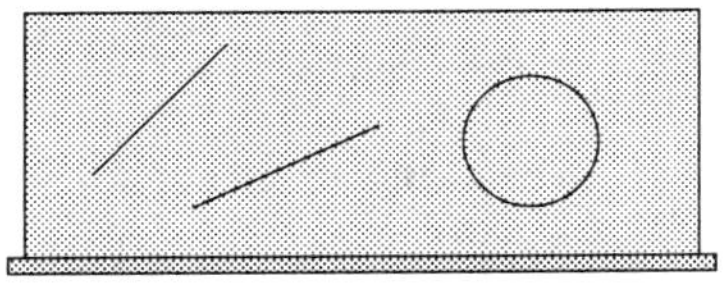

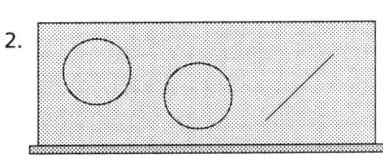

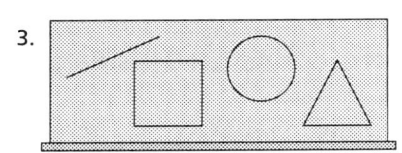

27

Look and Say

This exercise lets your children verbalize the words they have been hearing on the tape. And since they have to say the Latin words based solely on looking at the shapes (rather than just reading Latin words), it also tests their actual knowledge of the words.

Instructions for This Page

Have your children point to the first four shapes and tell you the names of the shapes in Latin. Next have your children describe what is drawn on each chalkboard.

Encourage your children to use both Latin shape names and Latin numbers in describing the contents of the chalkboards.

Have your children pause the tape as needed to have time to give their answers.

💡 Have your children come up with their own order of shapes and draw them on new "chalkboards." This will encourage them to internalize the language and to develop their own creativity.

Audio Transcript

Narrator: Look at the shapes on your activity book page. As you point to each shape, say what its name is in Latin.

Number 1. It's *unus circulus*. Did you say *unus circulus*? That's right.

Number 2. *Unum quadratum.*

Number 3. *Unum triangulum.*

Number 4. *Una linea.*

Now chalkboards. Say what you see on each of the chalkboards.

Number 5. *Duae lineae et unus circulus.*

Number 6. *Duo circuli et una linea.*

Number 7. *Una linea, unum quadratum, unus circulus et unum triangulum.*

Lines and Figures — Look and Say

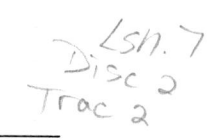

At the Village Market

This section contains an audio transcript of the adventure story your children will hear on the tape.

Instructions for This Page

Have your children listen carefully as the adventure story is read on the tape. Encourage your children to take an active part in listening to the adventure story. Ask them to respond to things they hear and have them say out loud words said by the characters on the tape.

Younger children might enjoy coloring the picture as the adventure story is read. Older children may want to follow along with the written audio transcript provided in this *Parent's Guide*.

Audio Transcript

Narrator 2: The Adventure Continues: At the Market

Narrator: After learning the Latin words for some of the marks and shapes on Marcus' map, you get up and continue on your way through the jungle. After an hour or two of good hiking, you come out of the towering trees and thick vegetation at the edge of a village. There are lots of huts like the one Marcus lives in, and in the middle of the village there is a market with dozens of stands where people are selling food, clothes, cookware, and lots of other things. Marcus leads you right into the middle of the stands. People are bustling all around you, buying and selling a thousand different goods.

Jill: This is so exciting—a real open-air market!

Henry: Yeah! Look at all the different kinds of fruits and vegetables and stuff. I bet we could find almost anything here.

Marcus: Let's buy some food at this stand here. I've had it before, it's really good.

Narrator: You buy plenty of food for a picnic lunch, and while you eat you continue to take in the sights and sounds of the marketplace. "There are so many colors here!" you exclaim.

Jill: Yeah. I especially love the variety of clothing. Marcus, can you teach us Latin words for different colors?

Marcus: Sure. That's a great idea, Jill.

Lsn. 7
Disc 2
Trac 3

Power-Glide **Children's Latin**

Colors at the Market

This exercise introduces the Latin words for basic colors: white, black, red, green, yellow, blue, orange, brown, purple and pink.

In this exercise, your children are asked to color soda bottles in the different colors in order to help them connect the Latin words with the various colors. Once the bottles are colored, your children are asked to point to the colors (in Latin) which they hear on the tape. This reinforces the Latin color names in their minds.

Instructions for This Page

Have your children use crayons, markers or colored pencils to color in the bottles as the tape directs them. The two bottles in the top row are already colored white and black. Once the bottles are all colored, have your children point to each colored bottle as the tape directs them.

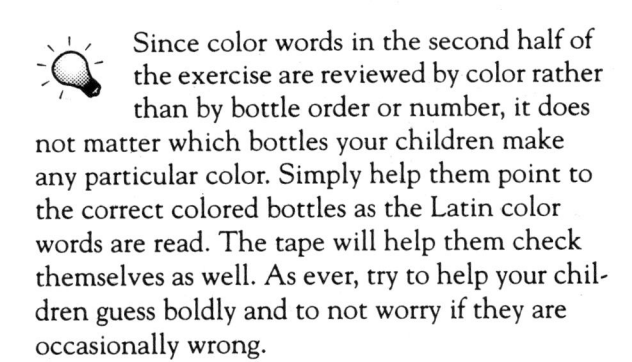

Since color words in the second half of the exercise are reviewed by color rather than by bottle order or number, it does not matter which bottles your children make any particular color. Simply help them point to the correct colored bottles as the Latin color words are read. The tape will help them check themselves as well. As ever, try to help your children guess boldly and to not worry if they are occasionally wrong.

Audio Transcript

Narrator 2: Activity: Colors at the Market.

Narrator: Marcus decides to give you a tour of the marketplace and teach you the Latin words for colors at the same time. First he takes you to a soda stand, with sodas of many different colors stacked in bottles for

Corresponding Page from Children's Activity Book

Colors at the Market
Color the sodas at the market

white   black

red   green   yellow   blue

orange   brown   purple   pink

30

people to buy. The bottles on your activity book page are like the ones you see at the market stand, only the ones on your page aren't colored yet.

To make your bottles look like the ones you see at the market, take out some crayons or markers or colored pencils. You will need these colors: red, green, yellow, blue, orange, black, brown, purple and pink, and white. A box of sixteen crayons or markers should have all of those. You may stop the tape if you need to get some.

Have you got something now to color with? Good! Let's begin. As I say the English and Latin words for a color, pick any one of the empty white bottles on your activity book page and color it in with that color. Stop the tape as often as you need to in order to have time to color. Are you ready? OK. Here we go.

The first soda Marcus points to is a strawberry flavor. It is bright red! So, pick one of the bottles on your page, and color it bright red! Are

Colors at the Market   **Colors at the Market**

Continued from Children's Activity Book, page 30

you finished? Good! The Latin word for red is *ruber*. That's easy to remember, isn't it? Say it out loud: *ruber*.

The next bottle is a white bottle of milk. It is all white. Color one of your bottles white. Marcus points to the bottle of milk and says: *albus*. Say it out loud. *Albus*. That means "white" in Latin.

The next bottle Marcus points to has black cherry flavored soda in it. It is black. Color one of your bottles black. The Latin word for "black" is *niger*. Say it out loud. *Niger*.

The next flavor of soda Marcus points to is lime. It is a delicious looking green color. Pick one of your bottles, and color it green. Are you finished? Good! The Latin word for green is *viridis*. Can you remember that? Say it out loud: *viridis*.

After that, Marcus points to a lemon flavored soda. It is colored yellow, *flavus*. Say it out loud: *flavus*. Now color one of your bottles *flavus*. Are you finished coloring one of the bottles yellow? Good.

Next Marcus points to a blue colored soda. It is some kind of fruit punch. He tells you that the Latin word for blue is *caeruleus*. Say it out loud: *caeruleus*. So, pick another bottle and color it *caeruleus*—color it blue. Are you finished? Good.

The next bottle Marcus points to has orange flavor soda in it. Can you guess what color it is? That's right! It is orange! That was too easy! The Latin word for orange is *luteus*. Pick another empty bottle and color it orange—color it *luteus*. Are you finished? Good.

After showing you the orange soda, Marcus points to a cola drink. It is brown. Pick one of your bottles and color it brown. Are you finished? Good! The Latin word for brown is *fuscus*. Can you say that? *Fuscus*. *Fuscus*.

The second to last soda Marcus points to is grape flavored—purple. He tells you the Latin word for purple is *purpureus*. *Purpureus*. So, pick one of the bottles you haven't colored yet, and color it *purpureus*—purple. Are you finished? Good.

The last soda bottle is full of pink lemonade. Marcus points to it and says: *roseus, roseus*. *Roseus* means pink! That one is easy to remember because it sounds like a rose, and lots of roses are pink. So, color the last bottle *roseus*. Are you finished? Excellent!

Well, you should have all the bottles colored in now. That's a lot of colors to learn, isn't it? You aren't sure you'll ever be able to remember them, but Marcus helps you. He says the Latin words for the colors and lets you point to the soda you think it is. Let's do the same thing together. I'll say a color in Latin, and you try to point to the right colored soda bottle on your activity book page. Ready? OK, here goes.

Viridis, viridis. Point to the soda you colored *viridis*. Did you point to the green soda? Good! Now another.

Caeruleus. Point to the soda you colored *caeruleus*. Did you point to the blue soda? Good. Now another.

Flavus. Point to the soda you colored *flavus*. Did you point to the yellow soda? That's right. Now another.

Ruber. Point to the soda you colored *ruber*. Did you point to the red soda? Well done. Now another.

Roseus. Point to the soda you colored *roseus*. Did you point to the pink soda? Good. Now another.

Fuscus. Point to the soda you colored *fuscus*. Did you point to the brown soda? Right again. Now another.

Luteus. Point to the soda you colored *luteus*. Did you point to the orange soda? Good. Now one more.

Purpureus. Point to the soda you colored *purpureus*. Did you point to the purple soda? Well done.

Power-Glide **Children's Latin**

Scatter Chart

This exercise continues to teach Latin colors by having your children identify and color fruits, vegetables and other things at the market that are the different colors they have learned.

Instructions for This Page

As colors are said on the tape, have your children use crayons, markers or colored pencils to color in the appropriate item.

Audio Transcript

Narrator: Once he has taught you the colors at the soda stand, Marcus takes you around the market, telling you colors and asking you to find things that are those colors. For example, he starts by asking you to find something that is *albus*, something that is white. You only have to look for a minute to find a man selling milk. Milk is *albus*!

Let's practice. As I say a color in Latin, find one of the pictures on your activity book page that is of something which is usually that color. Are you ready? OK. Find something on this page that is usually *flavus*. Did you pick the banana? Good! Bananas are usually yellow, *flavus*, aren't they? Go ahead and color the banana *flavus*—yellow. Are you finished coloring the banana *flavus*? Good. Now let's try another color.

Try to find something on this page that is usually *viridis*. Can you see anything that is usually *viridis*? I see something—the lettuce! Lettuce is usually *viridis*, isn't it? So, go ahead and color the lettuce *viridis*—green. Are you finished coloring? Good.

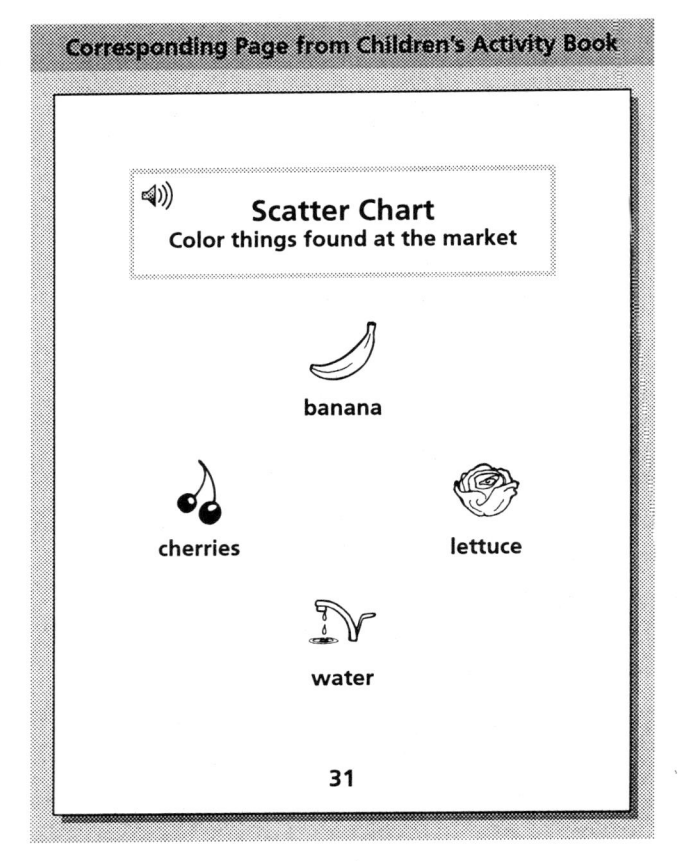

Corresponding Page from Children's Activity Book

Scatter Chart
Color things found at the market

banana

cherries   lettuce

water

31

Now look at your page and see if there is anything on it that is usually *ruber*. What do you think? Is it the cherries? I'd say so! Cherries are usually very *ruber*-colored, very red-colored. So, go ahead and color the cherries *ruber*. Are they colored *ruber* now? Good job.

The last thing on your page is some water. Can you guess what color water is, like in the ocean, or in a lake? That's right! It's blue—*caeruleus*! When Marcus asks you to find a fruit or vegetable that was *caeruleus*, you can't see any, so you point out to the water in the ocean—that is very *caeruleus*—very blue! So, color the water *caeruleus*—color it blue. Are you finished? Good.

Match and Learn

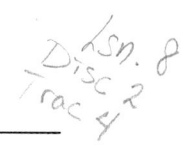

This exercise tests your children on the four colors reviewed in the previous exercise. Your children are asked to point to the correct items based solely on their color names in Latin.

Instructions for This Page

Have your children point to the items in the various frames that are the colors said on the tape. For instance, when the tape says to point to the item in frame 1 that is *flavus*—yellow, your children should point to the box in that frame which is yellow—the banana.

Have your children pause the tape as needed to have time to give their answers.

Audio Transcript

Narrator: Now that you've learned a few of the Latin words for colors, let's see which ones you can remember. As I say a color in Latin, point to the thing in your activity book which is that color. For example, when I say point to something that is *viridis*, you point to the lettuce, because it is green. Are you ready? OK, here goes.

Look at the large frame on your activity book page. Point to the thing that is *ruber*. Did you point to the cherries? Good! That's right! A cherry is *ruber*—it is red! Now point to the thing that is *flavus*. Did you point to the banana? Well done! The banana is *flavus*—yellow. Now point to the thing that is *caeruleus*. Did you choose the water? Good! The water is blue—*caeruleus*!

Now look at the numbered shapes at the bottom of your page. As I say what each thing is, say out loud what color it is in Latin!

Here we go:

Corresponding Page from Children's Activity Book

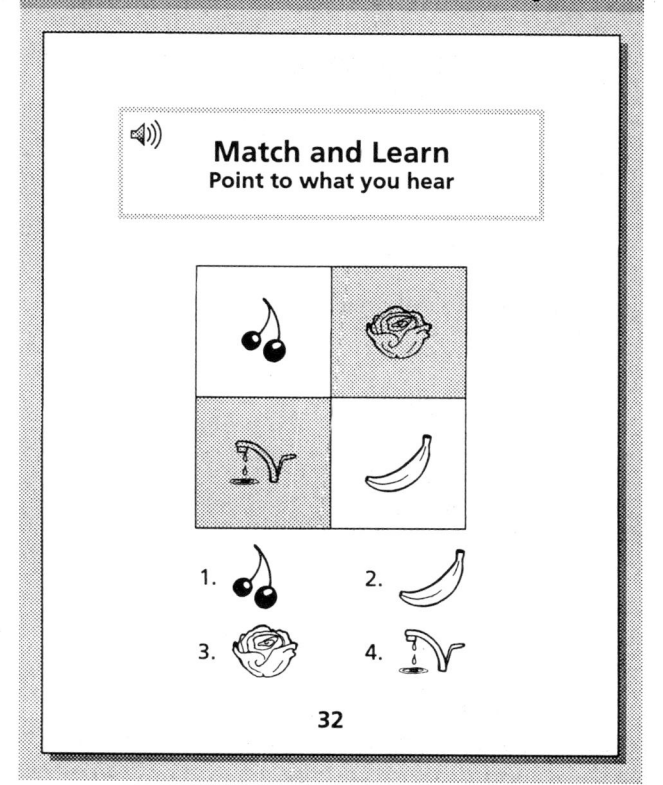

Match and Learn
Point to what you hear

Number 1: A couple of cherries. Did you say *ruber*? That's right! Cherries are *ruber* color—they are red color!

Number 2: A banana. Did you say *flavus*? Yes, bananas are *flavus* color.

Number 3: A head of lettuce. Did you say *viridis*? Good.

Number 4: Water. Did you say *caeruleus*? Good.

Colors at the Market — Match and Learn

Scatter Chart

This exercise continues to teach Latin colors by having your children identify and color fruits, vegetables and other things at the market that are the different colors they have learned.

Instructions for This Page

As a color is said on the tape, have your children use crayons, markers or colored pencils to color in the appropriate item.

Audio Transcript

Narrator: You did a great job remembering those colors. Now let's try to find things that are some other colors.

The next color Marcus asks you to find is *purpureus*. Can you see something on your page that is often *purpureus*—often purple? The grapes? Right! You look around the market and find some purple grapes. There are other grapes that are *viridis*, but the ones you pick are *purpureus*. So, take out your colors, and make the grapes purple! Are you finished? Good!

The next color Marcus asks you to find is *fuscus*—something that is *fuscus* color. See if you can find something on your page that is usually *fuscus*. Did you pick the potato? Nice work! Potatoes are usually *fuscus* color, aren't they? They are usually brown. So, color the potato on your page *fuscus*.

Next, Marcus asks you to look for something *luteus*. See if you can find something on your page that is usually *luteus*. Is a carrot usually *luteus*? Yes, a carrot usually is *luteus*—it usually is orange! So, color the carrot on your page *luteus*.

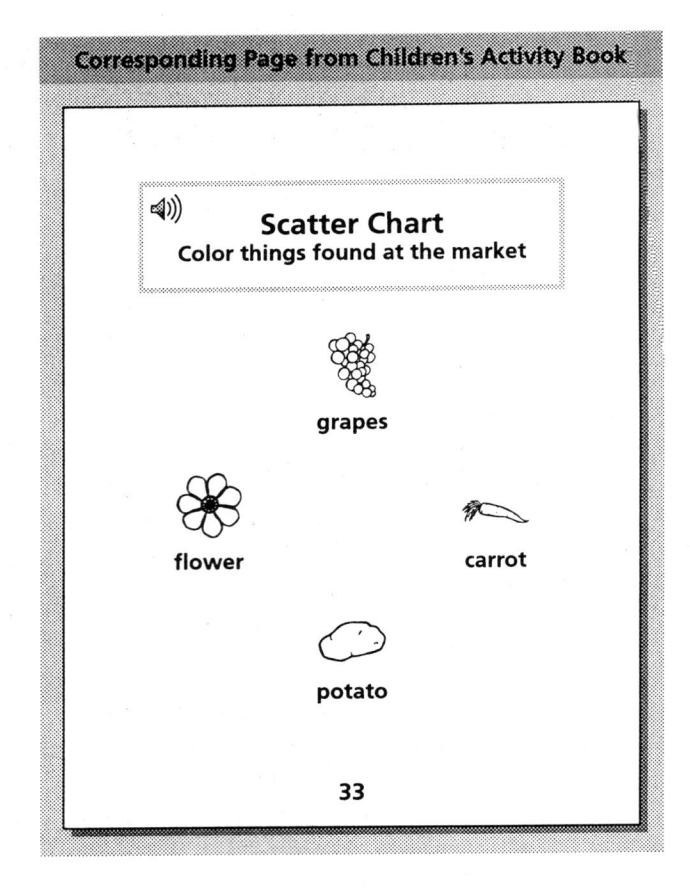

Corresponding Page from Children's Activity Book

Scatter Chart
Color things found at the market

grapes

flower   carrot

potato

33

The last thing on your page is a flower. Do you remember the Latin word for pink? That's right! It's *roseus*. Marcus asks you to find something at the market that is *roseus*, and you find a beautiful flower. It is the pinkest thing you've ever seen! So, color the flower on your page *roseus*.

Power-Glide **Children's Latin**

Match and Learn

This exercise tests your children on the four colors reviewed in the previous exercise. Your children are asked to point to the correct items based solely on their color names in Latin.

Instructions for This Page

Have your children point to the items in the various frames that are the colors said on the tape. For instance, when the tape says to point to the item in frame 1 that is *fuscus*—brown, your children should point to the box in that frame which is brown—the potato.

Have your children pause the tape as needed to have time to give their answers.

Audio Transcript

Narrator: Now that you've learned a few more of the Latin words for colors, let's see which ones you can remember. As I say a color in Latin, point to the thing in your activity book which is that color. For example, when I say point to something that is *fuscus*, you would point to the potato, because it is brown—*fuscus*. Are you ready? OK, here goes.

Look at the large frame on your activity book page. Point to the thing that is *purpureus*. Did you point to the grapes? Good! That's right! Grapes are *purpureus* in color—they are purple! Now point to the thing that is *luteus*. Did you point to the carrot? Well done! Carrots are *luteus* color, aren't they? Now point to the thing that is *roseus*. Did you choose the flower? Good! The flower is pink, *roseus* color!

Now look at the numbered shapes at the bottom of your page. As I say what each thing is, say out loud what color it is in Latin!

Here we go:

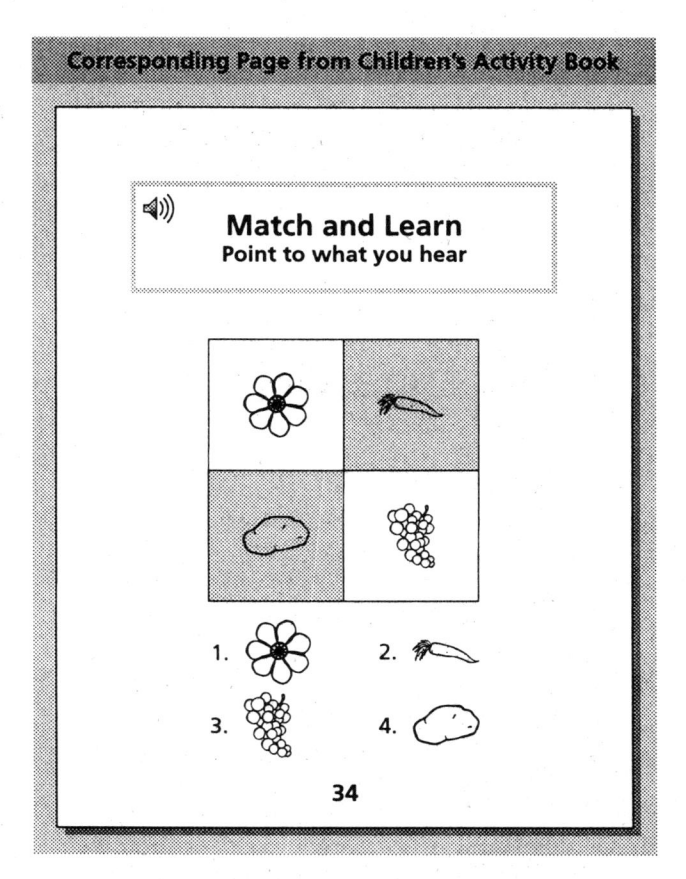

Corresponding Page from Children's Activity Book

Match and Learn
Point to what you hear

Number 1: A flower. Did you say *roseus*? That's right! A flower is *roseus* color—it is pink.

Number 2: A carrot. Did you say *luteus*? That's right! A carrot is *luteus* color.

Number 3: A bunch of grapes. Did you say *purpureus* color? Good!

Number 4: A potato. Did you say *fuscus*? Good!

Colors at the Market   P–45   Match and Learn

Match and Learn

This exercise tests your children on all of the colors learned in this activity. Your children are asked to point to the correct items based solely on their color names in Latin.

Instructions for This Page

Have your children point to the items in the various frames that are the colors said on the tape.

Audio Transcript

Narrator: Now that we've reviewed the Latin words for all the colors, let's see which ones you can remember. As I say a color in Latin, point to the thing in your activity book which is that color. For this exercise, you will also need to remember the Latin words for black and white. The Latin word for "black," if you remember, is *niger*. The Latin word for "white" is *albus*. *Niger* and *albus*. Black and white. Now are you ready to review all the colors? Good! As I say a color, point to the right item in each frame.

Look at frame 1. Point to the thing that is *purpureus*. Did you point to the grapes? Well done! Now point to the thing that is *albus*. Did you point to the white bottle? Good job! Now point to the thing that is *flavus*, *flavus* color. Did you choose the banana? Nice work. The last thing in this frame is a potato. Do you remember what color a potato is? That's right! It's *fuscus* color—brown.

Now look at frame 2. Can you see something here that is *ruber*? The cherries? Right! How about *luteus*? Can you see anything here that is *luteus* color? The carrot? Correct! And finally, do you see anything *roseus* color here?

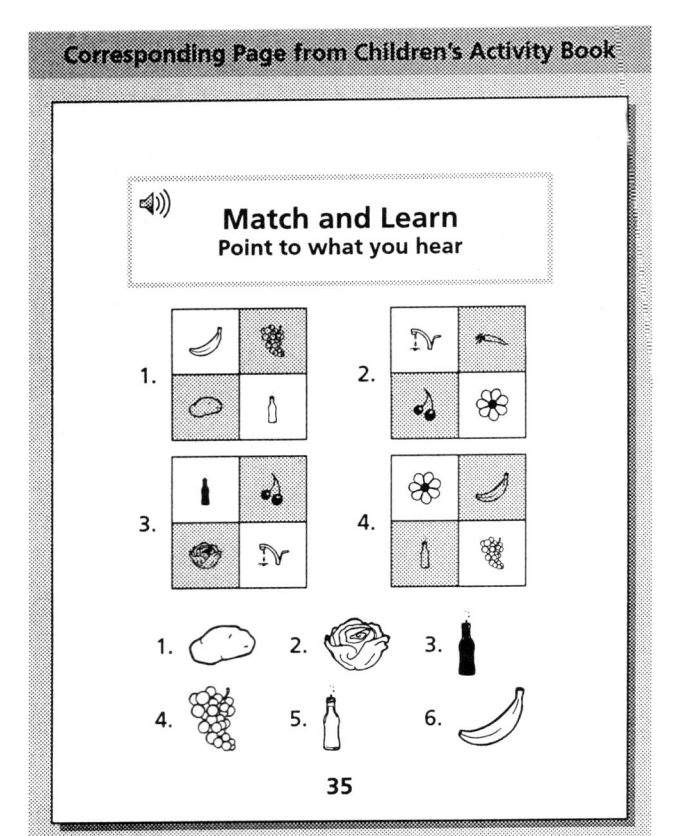

The flower? Exactly. The flower is *roseus* color. Good memory!

Now look at frame 3. Which of these things is *caeruleus*? Is it the lettuce? No, the lettuce is *viridis*! The water is *caeruleus*! Now, which thing is *ruber*? The cherries? Right on! And which thing is *niger*? The bottle? That's right! And finally, which thing is *viridis*? The lettuce? Of course! We just told you that! And you remembered anyway.

Now look at frame 4. Point to the thing that is *albus*. Did you point to the white bottle? Well done! Now, point to the thing that is *flavus* color. Did you choose the banana? Well done! And now, point to the thing that is *purpureus* color. The grapes, right? You've learned these colors very well.

Now look at the numbered shapes at the bottom of your page. As I say what each thing is, say out loud what color it is in Latin!

Colors at the Market · Match and Learn

Continued from Children's Activity Book, page 35

Here we go:

Number 1: A potato. Did you say *fuscus* color? That's right! A potato is *fuscus*—it is brown.

Number 2: A head of lettuce. Did you say *viridis*? That's right!

Number 3: A bottle of black cherry soda. Did you say *niger*? Excellent!

Number 4: A bunch of grapes. Did you say *purpureus*? Good!

Number 5: A white bottle of milk. Did you say *albus*? Well done!

Number 6: A banana. Did you say *flavus* color? Perfect!

You've learned your colors very well.

Meeting Claudia at the Market

This section contains an audio transcript of the adventure story your children will hear on the tape.

Instructions for This Page

Have your children listen carefully as the adventure story is read on the tape. Encourage your children to take an active part in listening to the adventure story. Ask them to respond to things they hear and have them say out loud words said by the characters on the tape.

Younger children might enjoy coloring the picture as the adventure story is read. Older children may want to follow along with the written audio transcript provided in this *Parent's Guide*.

Audio Transcript

Narrator 2: The Adventure Continues: Meeting Claudia at the Market

Jill: Wow, Marcus. This is fun.

Henry: Yeah, learning the Latin words for things right here around us is exciting. It kind of makes the language come alive.

Marcus: Good! I hope you will all start to love Latin as much as I do. And that's another key to learning it: make learning fun. If you get worried about not understanding everything at first, or about learning lots of new words at once, you won't do as well as if you just try to enjoy learning, and if you find ways to make learning fun.

Narrator: "That's a good tip, Marcus," you say. "Thank you for sharing it with us."

Corresponding Page from Children's Activity Book

The Adventure Continues
Meeting Claudia at the Market

Marcus: You're welcome. But right now, I need to get back home. And I can't leave you here without helping you find someone who can show you a way back to the other side of the island. Let's see if anyone knows about the mountain pass my father has told me about.

Jill: Good idea, Marcus. Thanks for staying a bit longer.

Narrator: So you go around the market, asking people if they are familiar with the pass that leads to the other side of the island. You're surprised by their response. "There is no pass," many people say, and "Why would you want to leave our side of the island, anyway?" others want to know. Finally, you meet a friendly woman who seems to have at least a hint of a solution to your problem, and who speaks some English.

Claudia: A mountain pass leading to the other side of the island, you say. Why do you seek such a place?

Adventure: Meeting Claudia at the Market Meeting Claudia at the Market

Continued from Children's Activity Book, page 37

Jill: Well, that's where we came from just yesterday, and the group we're with is leaving the island in less than a week, so we need to find a way back to them soon!

Claudia: Oh, I see. Well, I know a man who just might be able to help you. His name is Aeneas.

Marcus: Aeneas? Like the warrior who led the survivors of Troy on their journey to eventually build Rome?

Claudia: That's right! But the Aeneas I'm talking about is a banana farmer who lives in the foothills of the mountains here on our side of the island. The reason I think he might be able to help you is this: for years he has claimed to have been to the other side when he was just a boy. He insists that he got there by going through a secret pass high in the mountains at the middle of the island. So if you've heard of such a place, it's probably from a rumor that he started. And if there is any truth to the rumor, he might be just the person to guide you.

Henry: Great! Well, let's go meet him right away! Which house does he live in?

Claudia: Oh, I didn't say he lives here in town. He lives near the mountains, a few hours walk from here. I'll tell you what, why don't you stay at my home tonight, and in the morning I'll give you a map that will show you how to get to his house. Can you read maps?

Jill: You bet. Marcus even taught us the Latin words for lines and figures.

Claudia: Marvelous! Now, come with me to my home.

Narrator: This sounds like a good plan, and you all agree to it. Now that everything is settled, Marcus says:

Marcus: Well, I guess this is goodbye. I hope to someday see all of you again. *Valete*, you guys!

Henry: Thanks, Marcus!

Jill: Yeah. Thanks a lot. We wouldn't have ever gotten this far without you.

Narrator: You wave goodbye to Marcus as he heads back toward the jungle path and his family's home. Then you help Claudia close her stand, and before you know it, you are at her home enjoying a delicious supper of curry chicken, fried rice, green mangoes in pepper sauce, and sweet rice pudding for dessert. As you eat, you ask Claudia, "Claudia, when Marcus said goodbye this afternoon he said, '*Valete*' What does '*Valete*' mean?"

Claudia: Oh, It just means "goodbye." You say *valete* if you're saying goodbye to more than one person, that's why Marcus said *valete* when he said goodbye to the three of you. If you want to say goodbye to just one person you can shorten it to just *vale*.

Jill: Oh, so we should have said *Vale* back to Marcus!

Claudia: Yes, you could have. Here, let me teach you a little song to help you remember in the future. It goes:

<<<Tune: Good Night, Ladies!>>>

Valete, puellae,
Valete, puellae,
Valete, puellae
Et vobis gratias.

Now can you tell me what that means in English?

Narrator: "Well," you say, "*Valete* means 'goodbye.' You just told us that."

Henry: And *puellae* sounds like *puella*, and *puella* means "girl," Marcus told us a story that taught us that. I don't know what *puellae* means, though.

Claudia: It means "girls." That's why I said *valete* instead of *vale*. And the last line, *Et vobis gratias,* means, "And to you, thanks."

Adventure: Meeting Claudia at the Market   Meeting Claudia at the Market

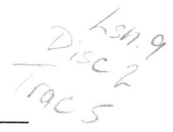

Continued from Children's Activity Book, page 37

Jill: OK, so in English the song is:

> Goodbye, girls,
> Goodbye, girls,
> Goodbye, girls,
> And to you thanks.

Claudia: Excellent, Jill. Now let's all sing it together.

Narrator: You sing along.

Claudia, Jill, Henry:

> *Valete, puellae,*
> *Valete, puellae,*
> *Valete, puellae*
> *Et vobis gratias.*

Henry: That's a good way to remember what *valete* means. But what would it be if we wanted to sing, "Farewell, boys"? The Latin word for boy is *puer*; Marcus taught us that, too. But I don't know how to say "boys."

Claudia: The Latin word for boys is *pueri*. Listen:

> *Valete pueri,*
> *Valete, pueri,*
> *Valete, pueri*
> *Ab omnibus idem.*

Henry: I get it. But what does it mean, *Ab omnibus idem*?

Claudia: It means, "From everyone the same." Let's sing the "Farewell boys" version together, too.

Claudia, Jill, Henry:

> *Valete, pueri,*
> *Valete, pueri,*
> *Valete, pueri*
> *Ab omnibus idem.*

Claudia: Wonderful! You are all learning Latin very quickly. Now we'd better stop singing for a bit and concentrate on eating!

Narrator: After you finish eating, you thank her several times.

Henry: That was excellent food, Claudia!

Jill: Yeah, you're a really good cook!

Claudia: Well thank you, children. But you haven't tried my specialty.

Narrator: "What's that?" you ask.

Claudia: Cookies! I love to bake cookies and pastries of all varieties. In fact, if you'd like, we could make a batch of my best cookies right now.

Jill: Alright!

Henry: Yes, please, let's do!

Claudia: OK, you children can help me measure out the ingredients.

Narrator: You have lots of fun helping Claudia measure and mix ingredients for cookies. When the dough is ready, you roll it out flat and use a cookie cutter to make it into shapes. The first batch you make look like gingerbread men, and twenty minutes later the cookies are done.

Henry: Mmmm! These are delicious, Claudia.

Jill: Uh-huh! Mmmm!

Claudia: Thank you. It is my best recipe, after all. And I have something else in mind for you, too.

Narrator: "What's that?" you ask.

Claudia: I will use these cookies to teach you some more Latin, words for parts of the body.

Henry: OK. That sounds fun!

Jill: Yeah!

Adventure: Meeting Claudia at the Market

Body Parts

This activity is designed to teach your children the Latin words for parts of the body. It incorporates kinesthetic associations, drawing and matching activities in going over the body part words several times.

This first exercise introduces the basic body parts.

Instructions for This Page

Have your children look at the picture of the gingerbread man cookie in their activity book and point to the parts of the cookie's body as the tape directs them.

> Encourage your children to say the Latin words out loud as they point to each body part.

Audio Transcript

Narrator 2: Activity: Body Parts.

Narrator: Here are the words for different parts of the body, the *corpus*, that Claudia teaches you! As I say the Latin word for each part, point to that part and repeat the Latin word. Ready? OK.

Here we go!

Point to the cookie's head. The Latin word for "head" is *caput*. Say it out loud while pointing at the head: *caput, caput*.

Now point to the cookie's body, or trunk. The "body" or "trunk" is called the *truncus*. Say it out loud: *truncus*.

Now point to the cookie's arm. An "arm" in Latin is called a *bracchium*. And two arms are called *bracchia*. Say those out loud: one *bracchium*, two *bracchia*. *Unum bracchium, duo bracchia.*

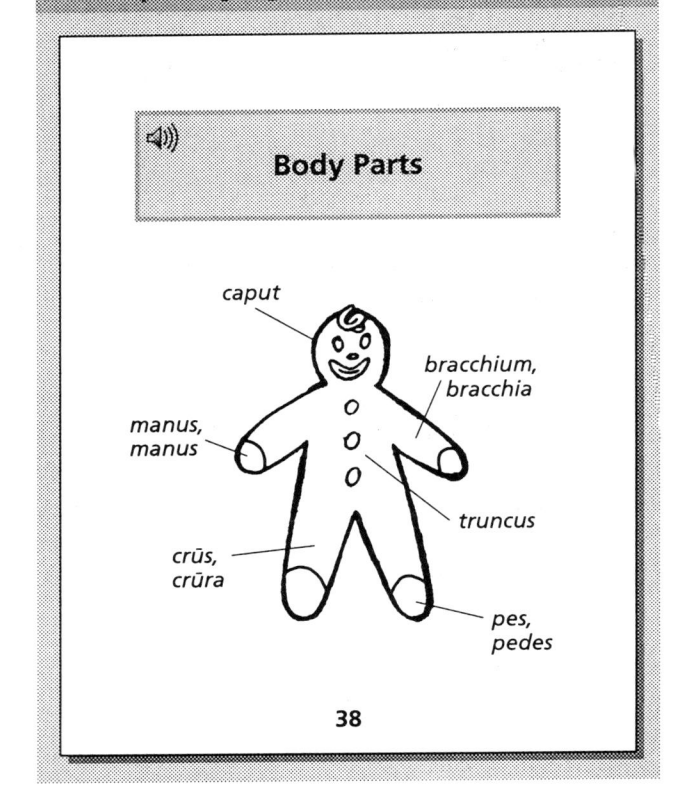

Now point to one of the cookie's hands. Are you pointing to a hand, a *manus*? Good! *Manus* is the Latin word for "hand," and "hands," meaning two hands, is also *manus*. Say *manus* out loud: *manus, manus*.

Now, point to one of the cookie's legs. Are you pointing to a leg, a *crūs*? Good. *Crūs* is the Latin word for "leg." Say it out loud: *crūs, crūs*. And the Latin word for two legs is *crūra*. Say it out loud: *crūra*. Say them out loud. One *crūs*, two *crūra*. *Unum crūs, duo crūra.*

Finally, point to one of the cookie's feet. In Latin "foot" is *pes*. Say *pes* out loud: *pes*. And two feet are called *pedes*. *Pedes*. Say those out loud. One *pes*, two *pedes*. *Unum pes, duo pedes.*

Did you point to each part and say the Latin word for it out loud? Good! Now you know the words for the basic parts of the body. As we go along, you'll learn them even better!

Power-Glide **Children's Latin**

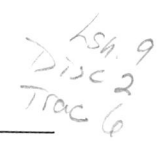

Match and Learn

This exercise reviews the basic body parts your children have just been introduced to by showing cookies with some parts missing (eaten) and asking them to point to the cookies with the specified missing parts.

Instructions for This Page

Have your children look at the pictures of partly eaten cookies and point to the ones with those missing parts indicated on the tape.

💡 A fun extension of this exercise would be to make cookies shaped like people and have your children say the name of each body part as they eat it—a good review and a yummy treat!

Audio Transcript

🔊 Narrator: To help you review the Latin words you have just learned, try looking at the partly eaten cookies on your activity book page and pointing to the ones I describe.

Point to the cookie without a *caput*. Did you point to the cookie without a head? Good.

Now point to the cookie that is missing one *bracchium*. Did you point to the cookie with only one arm? Good.

Now point to the cookie with no *manus* at all. Did you point to the one without any hands? Good.

Now find the cookie that has only one *crūs*. Did you find the one with only one leg? Good.

OK, now point to the cookie with a head, arms and legs, but no *truncus*. Did you pick the one without a body, or trunk? Good.

Corresponding Page from Children's Activity Book

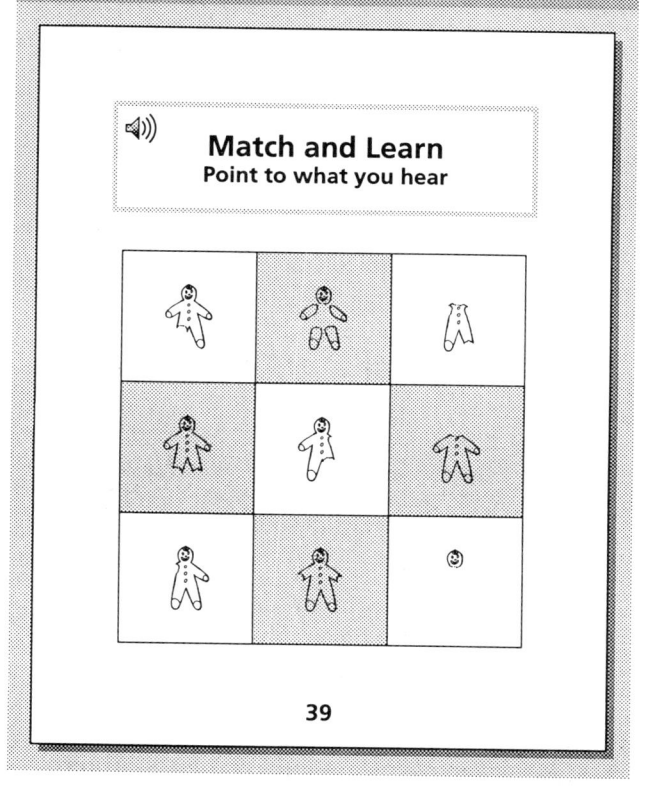

Match and Learn
Point to what you hear

39

Now point to the cookie with missing *pedes*. Did you point to the cookie that doesn't have any feet? Good.

Now find a cookie with only one *bracchium*, and only one *crūs*. Did you find the cookie with only one arm and only one leg? Good.

Now see if you can find a cookie with only one *pes*, no *caput*, and no *bracchia*. Did you find the one with only one foot, no head, and no arms? Good.

Finally, can you see a cookie with a *caput*, but no *corpus* to go with it? Did you pick the one that is just a head? That's the right one!

BODY PARTS — P–53 — Match and Learn

Draw and Learn

This exercise invites your children to draw a cookie of their own based on instructions given using Latin body part words.

Instructions for This Page

Have your children draw simple figures of their own, part by part as the tape directs. Have your children pause the tape as needed to have time for drawing.

Encourage your children to draw whatever kind of person they are comfortable with and interested in. For example, they can draw a cookie or a stick figure, a boy or a girl, a very simple figure or a more detailed, colorful one. Since the exercise is designed simply to reinforce their memory of the Latin words, let them do whatever makes it fun for them.

Audio Transcript

Narrator: Now that you know the Latin words for parts of the body, it's your turn to draw! Use a crayon, pencil, pen or marker to draw the parts of a person on the chalkboard as I say them in Latin. You can stop the tape and go get something to draw with if you need to. Are you ready to draw? All right, here we go!

First, draw a *caput*. Are you finished? Good!

Now, add to the *caput* a *truncus*. OK.

Now add *crūra* to the *truncus*.

And add *pedes* where they go.

Now add *bracchia* where they go.

Have you done all that? Good! What's left? *Manus*? Right!

Corresponding Page from Children's Activity Book

Draw and Learn
Draw what you hear

40

Add *manus* where they go. Done? All right. That should do it!

Now that your person is all drawn, fill it in or color it however you want. When you're done, turn the page to see an example of what you might have drawn.

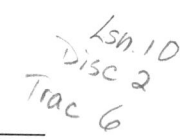

Draw and Learn

This page contains a sample drawing for your children to compare theirs to, and it also reinforces the Latin body part words.

Instructions for This Page

Have your children look at the picture of the gingerbread man cookie in their activity book and compare it to their drawing on the previous page. Have them look at the body parts as they are reviewed on the tape a final time.

If your children need more practice with the basic body parts, rewind the tape and let them try drawing figures a few more times.

Audio Transcript

Narrator: Here is a cookie that looks kind of like the one you just drew. It has all the body parts: a head—*a caput*, a body, or trunk—*a truncus*, legs—*crūra*, arms—*bracchia*, hands—*manus*, and feet—*pedes*. You can color this cookie now, if you like.

Corresponding Page from Children's Activity Book

41

Body Parts — Draw and Learn

Match and Learn

This exercise tests your children's memory of the Latin body part words learned so far.

Instructions for This Page

Have your children look at the Match and Learn frames and point to the appropriate pictures as the Latin words are read on the tape. Have your children pause the tape as needed to have time to give their answers.

Encourage your children to guess boldly in this exercise. If they guess wrong, they will usually have a chance to try again in a subsequent frame.

Audio Transcript

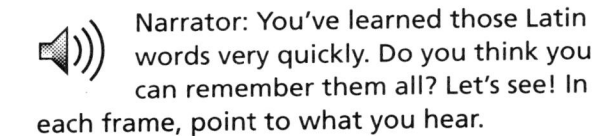

Narrator: You've learned those Latin words very quickly. Do you think you can remember them all? Let's see! In each frame, point to what you hear.

Look at frame 1. Point to the *manus*. Did you point to the hand? Good! Now point to the *caput*. Did you point to the head? Good! Finally, point to the *crūs*. Did you point to the leg? That's right.

Now look at frame 2. First, point to the *bracchium*. Did you point to the arm? That's right! Now point to the *truncus*. Did you point to the body, or trunk? Well done. Finally, point to the *pes*. Did you point to the foot? Good.

Now look at frame 3. Can you see a *crūs*? Did you choose the leg? That's right. Now, can you see a *caput*? Did you point to the head? Correct! And last, do you see a *manus* here? Yes? It's a hand, right?

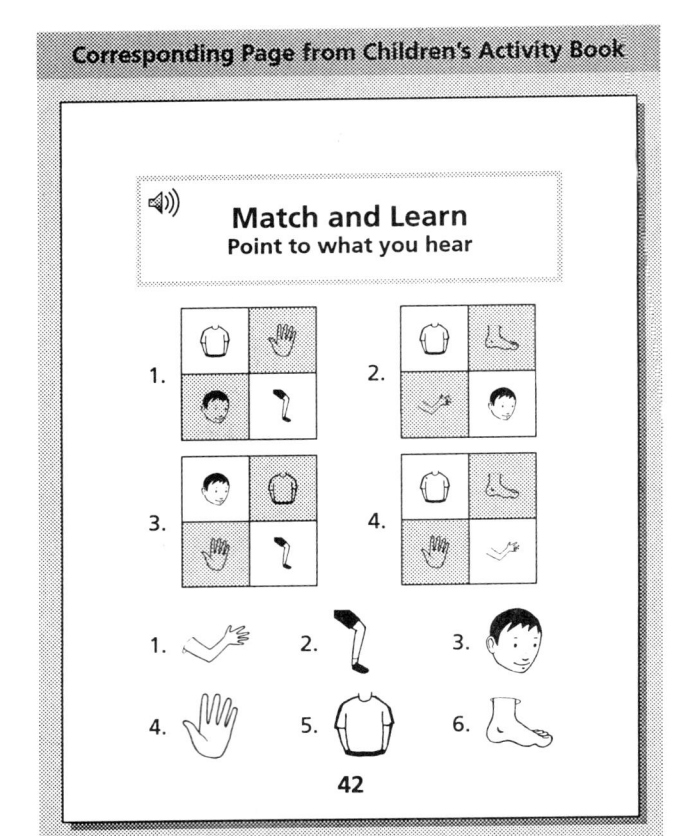

Now look at frame 4. Point to *the truncus*. Are you pointing to the body, or trunk? Now point to the *bracchium*. Did you point to the arm? Now point to the *pes*. Did you choose the foot? Good.

Now look at the numbered pictures at the bottom of the page. As I say the English word for each picture, say the Latin word for that picture out loud.

Number 1. Arm. Did you say *bracchium*? Good.

Number 2. Leg. Did you say *crūs*? Good.

Number 3. Head. Did you say *caput*? Good.

Number 4. Hand. Did you say *manus*? Good.

Number 5. Body, or trunk. Did you say *truncus*? Good.

Number 6. Foot. Did you say *pes*? Well done.

Draw and Learn

This exercise teaches your children the Latin word for fingers in a fun way by letting them trace around their own fingers.

Instructions for This Page

Have your children trace their hand in the chalkboard space on their activity book pages.

Audio Transcript

Narrator: Now that you know all those words, it is time for a new one: the Latin word for fingers. "Fingers" in Latin are called *digiti*. Each finger all by itself is called *digitus*. To help you learn this new word, I'd like you to trace your hand on the chalkboard on your page. This is easy to do, and you have probably even done it before. All you need to do is put your hand down on the page right in the middle of the chalkboard, and trace around it with a crayon or a pencil. Go ahead and trace your hand now.

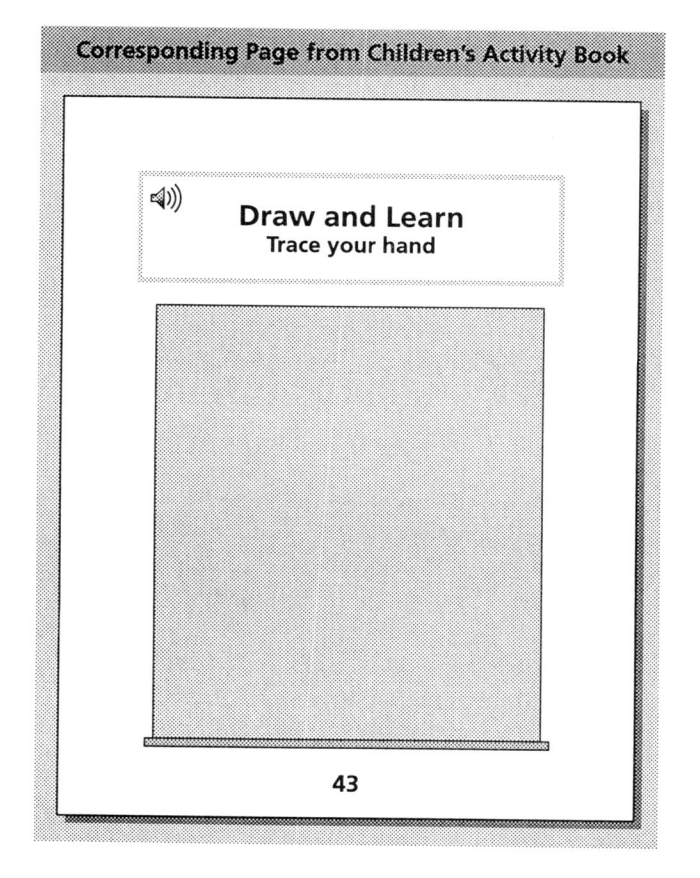

Corresponding Page from Children's Activity Book

Draw and Learn
Trace your hand

43

Draw and Learn

This page contains a sample of what your children's hand tracing may have looked like. This page also reinforces both the Latin word for fingers and the Latin numbers one through five by having your children count the fingers on the sample hand.

Instructions for This Page

Have your children compare their tracing to the sample on this page. Then have them point to the fingers one by one and count out loud as they are counted on the tape.

> If your children would like, they may turn back to the previous page and count the fingers of their own drawing.

Audio Transcript

Narrator: Are you finished? Good. Does your hand tracing look something like the one on this page? Yes? Wonderful! Now, let's learn more about fingers.

How many fingers—how many *digiti*—does your hand have? Five? That's right! Let's count the *digiti* in Latin. *Unus digitus, duo digiti, tres digiti, quattuor digiti, quinque digiti!* Let's count them one more time. *Unus digitus, duo digiti, tres digiti, quattuor digiti, quinque digiti!*

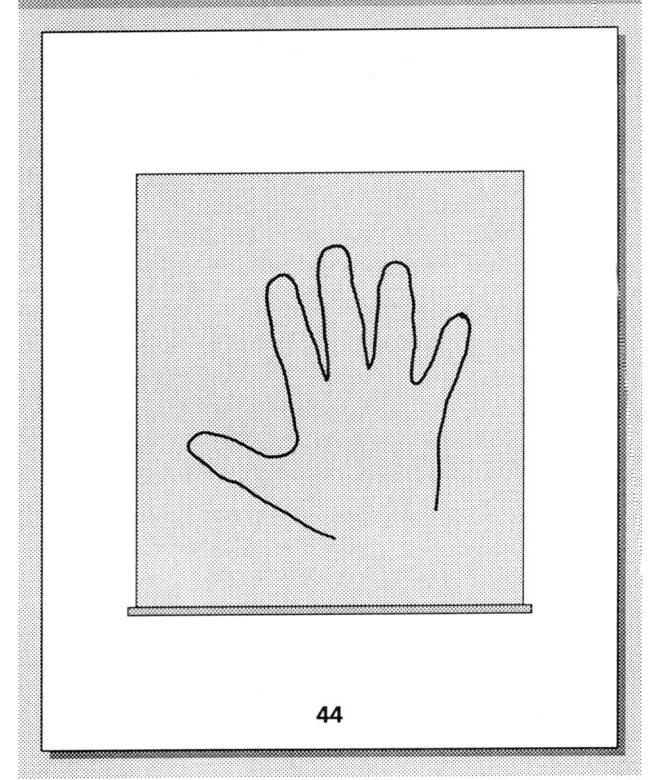

Face Parts

This next part of the activity is designed to teach your children the Latin words for parts of the face. The following exercises incorporate kinesthetic associations, drawing, matching and singing in going over the new words several times.

Instructions for This Page

Have your children look at the picture of the boy's face in their activity book and point to the parts of the face as the tape directs them.

💡 Encourage your children to say the Latin words out loud as they point to each part.

Audio Transcript

🔊 Narrator: Now that you know the Latin words for parts of your body, you're ready to learn the words for parts of your face. Look at the face of the boy on your activity book page and point to the different parts as I tell you their names in English and Latin.

Point to one of the boy's eyes. The Latin word for "eye" is *oculus*. Say it out loud while pointing to one eye: *oculus*. Eyes, as in two eyes, is *oculī*: *Oculī*.

Now point to the boy's nose. The word for "nose" in Latin is *nasus*. Say it out loud: *nasus*.

Now point to one of the boy's ears. The Latin word for "ear" is *auris*. Say *auris*. Two ears is just *aures*: *Aures*.

Now point to the boy's mouth—his *ōs*. *Ōs* is the Latin word for mouth. Say: *ōs, ōs*.

Corresponding Page from Children's Activity Book

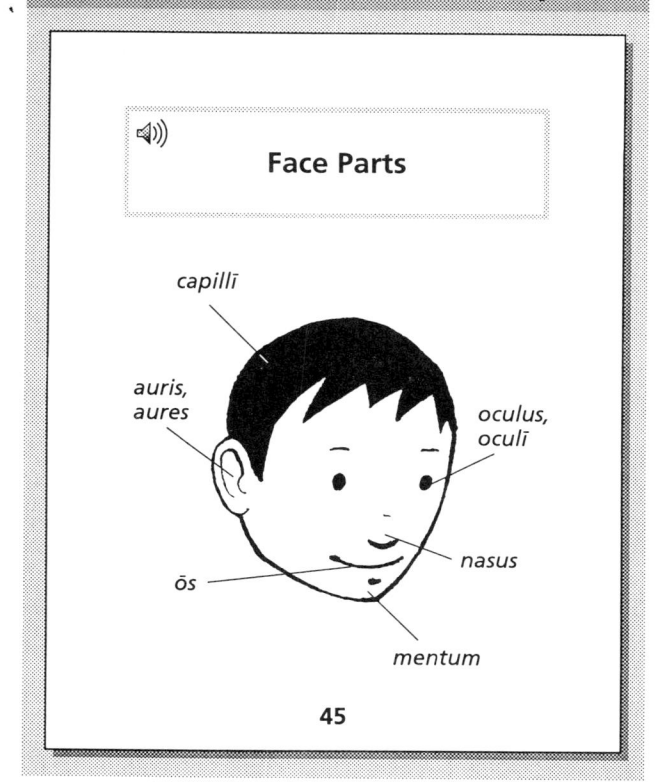

🔊 Face Parts

capillī
auris, aures
oculus, oculī
ōs
nasus
mentum

45

Now point to the boy's hair. The Latin word for hair is *capillī*. *Capillī* means hair. Say: *capillī*.

Now point to the boy's chin. The Latin word for "chin" is *mentum*. Say: *mentum*.

Can you remember all those? I'll go through them quickly one more time. Point to what you hear. First, the *oculī*—eyes. Next, the *nasus*—the nose. Now the *aures*—ears, and the *ōs*—the mouth. Now the *capillī*—hair; and finally, the *mentum*, the chin. Did you point to each one? Very good!

Draw and Learn

This exercise is designed to reinforce the Latin words for parts of the face in a fun way by having your children draw them.

Instructions for This Page

Have your children draw parts of the face on the oval shown in their work book as the tape directs them. Have your children pause the tape as needed to have time for drawing.

Encourage your children to be creative and draw whatever type of face they want, provided the parts are those called for on the tape.

Audio Transcript

Narrator: Now that you've learned those words, let's try drawing a face. On your activity book page there is a blank face ready to color on. As I say the words in Latin, draw the things I say on the blank face. Are you ready to draw? OK!

First draw an *ōs* on the face. Are you finished? Good. Did you draw a mouth? That's right!

Now draw *duo oculī* on the face. Are you finished? Did you draw two eyes? Good!

Now draw *aures* where they go. Did you draw ears on the sides? Good.

Now drawn a *nasus* on the face. Does your face have a nose now? Good.

Now draw *capillī* where it goes. Did you draw hair? That's right!

And that's all, except, of course, for the *mentum*—but the face already has a kind of *mentum*! (You can draw a better one if you want to.)

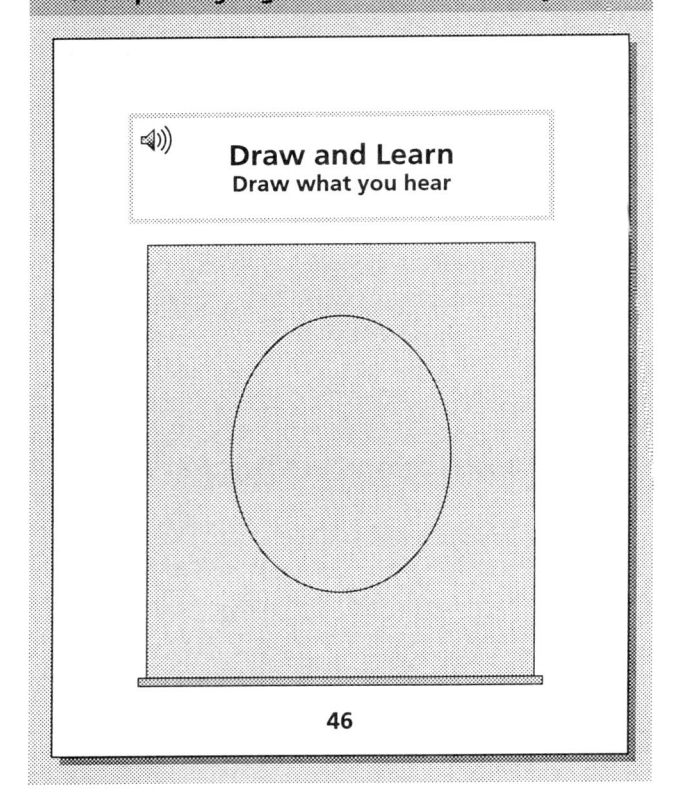

Match and Learn

This exercise tests your children's memory of the Latin face part words they have learned.

Instructions for This Page

Have your children look at the Match and Learn frames and point to the appropriate pictures as the Latin words are read on the tape.

Encourage your children to guess boldly in this exercise. If they guess wrong, they will usually have a chance to try again in a subsequent frame.

Audio Transcript

Narrator: You've learned those Latin words very quickly. Do you think you can remember them all? Let's see! In each frame, point to what you hear.

Look at frame 1. Point to the *mentum*. Did you point to the chin? Good! Now point to the *oculus*. Did you point to the eye? Good. Finally, point to the *auris*. Did you point to the ear? Well done.

Now look at frame 2. First, point to the *ōs*. Did you point to the mouth? Now point to the *nasus*. Did you point to the nose? Good. Finally, point to the *capillī*. Did you point to the hair? Good.

Now look at frame 3. Point to an *auris*. Did you point to the ear? Point to an *oculus*. Did you point to the eye? Good. Last, do you see a *mentum* here? It's a chin, isn't it?

Now look at frame 4. Point to the *manus* with *tres digiti* up. Are you pointing to the hand with three fingers up? Now point to the *manus* with *quinque digiti* up. Did you point to the hand with all five fingers up? Very good. Now point to the *manus* with *quattuor digiti* up. Did you choose the one with four fingers up? That's right!

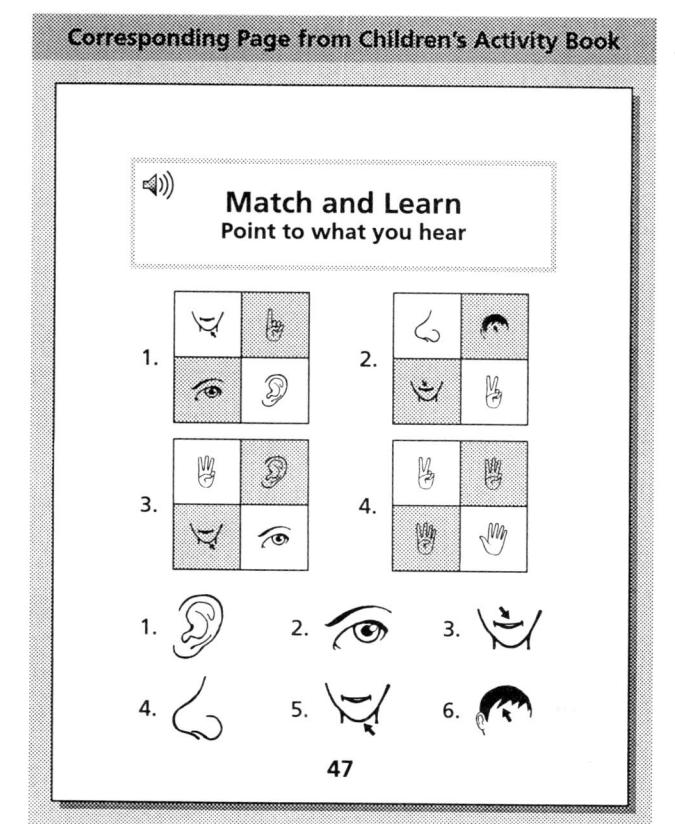

Now look at the numbered pictures at the bottom of the page. As I say the English word for each picture, say the Latin word for that picture out loud.

Number 1. Ear. Did you say *auris*? Good.

Number 2. Eye. Did you say *oculus*? Good.

Number 3. Mouth. Did you say *ōs*? Good.

Number 4. Nose. Did you say *nasus*? Good.

Number 5. Chin. Did you say *mentum*? Good.

Number 6. Hair. Did you say *capillī*? That's exactly right.

Touch and Learn

This exercise tests and reinforces your children's memory of the Latin body part and face part words they have learned by having them touch those parts of their own bodies and faces.

Instructions for This Page

Have your children listen to the Latin words said on the tape and touch the parts of their bodies and faces that the tape directs.

Encourage your children to stand up and have fun with this exercise. Encourage them to guess boldly.

Audio Transcript

Narrator: You've now learned the Latin words for all the main parts of your body and your face. Do you think you can remember them all? Let's see! Stand up, and as I say the Latin word for a part of your body or your face, touch it. For example, if I say: "Touch your *caput*," you should touch your head.

Let's try a few.

Touch your *nasus*. Did you touch your nose? Good.

Now touch your *bracchia*. Did you touch your arms? That's right.

Now touch your *pedes*. Did you touch your feet? Good.

Now touch your *truncus*. Did you touch your body, or trunk? Good job.

Now touch your *ōs*. Did you touch your mouth? Right.

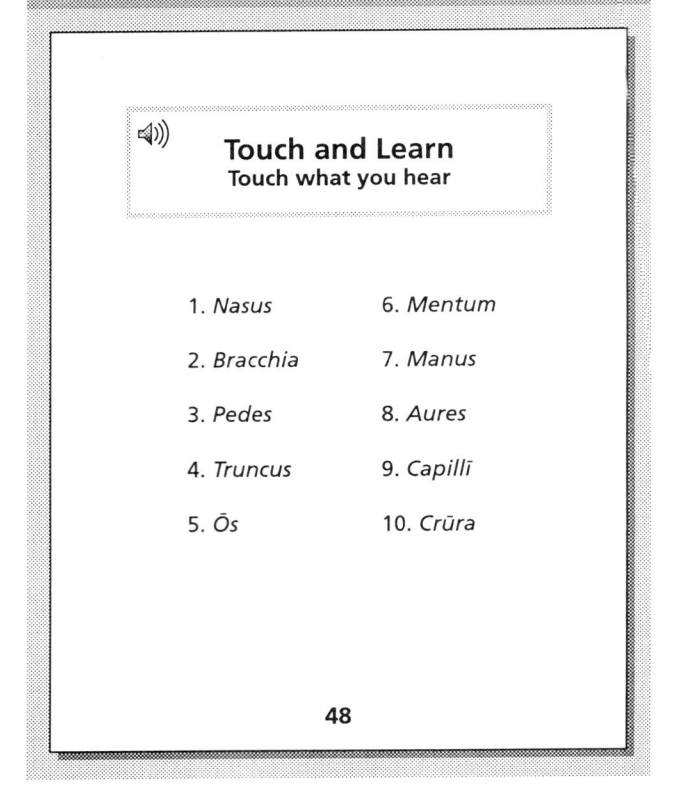

Now touch your *mentum*. Did you touch your chin! Good.

Now touch your *manus*. Did you touch your *manus* with your *manus*? I'll bet you did! Your *manus* are your hands, right?

Now touch your *aures*. Did you touch your ears? Good.

Now touch your *capillī*. Did you touch your hair? Right on.

Now touch your *crūra*. Did you touch your legs? Excellent!

Corresponding Page from Children's Activity Book

Touch and Learn
Touch what you hear

1. *Nasus*
2. *Bracchia*
3. *Pedes*
4. *Truncus*
5. *Ōs*
6. *Mentum*
7. *Manus*
8. *Aures*
9. *Capillī*
10. *Crūra*

48

Power-Glide **Children's Latin**

Sing and Learn

In this exercise your children use the words they have learned to sing an action song. This reinforces the words in their memory one last time, and makes learning them fun.

Instructions for This Page

Have your children listen to the song on the tape once completely through, then on the second, third and fourth times, have them try to sing along and touch the body parts sung in the song.

💡 Many children enjoy action songs very much, and they are one of the best ways to reinforce words in memory. Encourage your children to make up their own body parts songs!

Audio Transcript

🔊 Narrator: Now that you've learned the Latin words for all those parts of your body, you're ready to sing a song using them. The first time through, just listen to the song and think of the body parts that the words stand for. Then the second time through stand up and try to sing along and touch the parts of your body as you say them. Start out singing the song slowly, and then speed up until, on the third or fourth time, you're singing it as fast as you can!

The song goes like this. Remember, just listen this first time.

Caput, truncus, crūra, pedes,
    crūra, pedes, crūra, pedes,
Caput, truncus, crūra, pedes,
Oculī, aures, nasus et ōs.

Now stand up and try to sing along and touch the right parts of your body as you sing the words for them in the song! This time we will sing the song together slowly.

Caput, truncus, crūra, pedes,
    crūra, pedes, crūra, pedes,
Caput, truncus, crūra, pedes,
Oculī, aures, nasus et ōs.

How did you do? Were you able to keep up? Now again, a little faster:

Caput, truncus, crūra, pedes,
    crūra, pedes, crūra, pedes,
Caput, truncus, crūra, pedes,
Oculī, aures, nasus et ōs.

Did you keep up that time too? Wow, you're quick! All right, one more time, really fast.

Caput, truncus, crūra, pedes,
    crūra, pedes, crūra, pedes,
Caput, truncus, crūra, pedes,
Oculī, aures, nasus et ōs.

Wow! That was fast. I'm tired—how about you? Well, now you know an easy way to remember some of the Latin words you've just learned.

Corresponding Page from Children's Activity Book

🔊 **Sing and Learn**
Do the actions as you sing

Caput, truncus, crūra, pedes,

crūra, pedes, crūra, pedes,

Caput, truncus, crūra, pedes,

Oculī, aures, nasus et ōs.

49

Body Parts — Sing and Learn

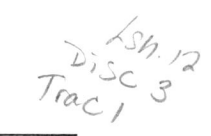

The Search for Aeneas

This section contains an audio transcript of the adventure story your children will hear on the tape.

Instructions for This Page

Have your children listen carefully as the adventure story is read on the tape. Encourage your children to take an active part in listening to the adventure story. Ask them to respond to things they hear and have them say out loud words said by the characters on the tape.

💡 Younger children might enjoy coloring the picture as the adventure story is read. Older children may want to follow along with the written audio transcript provided in this *Parent's Guide*.

Audio Transcript

🔊 Narrator 2: The Adventure Continues: The Search for Aeneas

Claudia: You children are very good learners.

Jill: Thanks, Claudia. Like Marcus taught us, it's easy to learn when you make learning fun!

Narrator: "That's right," you agree.

Henry: <yawns> Boy, I'm tired again. We've done lots of things today.

Jill: Yeah. I'm pretty tired too. Do you have any hammocks for us to sleep in, Claudia?

Claudia: Hammocks? Oh, no. But I do have some nice beds that are just your size. I had them made for when my nieces and nephews come to visit me. You'll love them.

Narrator: Soon you are all asleep. The next morning you wake up refreshed and excited to continue your adventure. Over breakfast Claudia gives you directions for the next stage of your journey.

Claudia: Now, to get to Aeneas' house you'll have to hike through the jungle again. Here is a map to show you the way. Don't take too long, or you'll get caught in the jungle in the dark. Also, don't stray off the path. If you do, you'll probably never find it again. Do you understand?

Jill: I think so.

Claudia: Good. You'll be safe enough if you just keep on. Now, here's food to eat when you stop to rest.

Henry: Thanks a lot, Claudia. You've been really nice to us.

Claudia: Oh, you're quite welcome, Henry. I hope very much indeed that Aeneas will be able to help you. He knows the mountains

Continued from Children's Activity Book, page 51

much better than any of us that live here in the village. And, although I've never been myself to the mountain pass he talks about, I've known Aeneas for many years, and I have never known him to tell a lie.

Narrator: After thanking Claudia one last time for her help, and for all the food she has packaged up to send with you, you and Jill and Henry begin your trek toward the mountains and Aeneas, the mysterious man you hope will become your guide.

At first your way is easy, as you walk through the village and along a wide road used by farmers and others bringing goods to the market. But then your map leads you off the road and along a winding jungle path that should lead you to Aeneas' home. As you enter the shadow of the trees, you feel the warmth of the jungle settle in around you, and you hear the same eerie jungle sounds that you heard on your hike into the village the day before. Not far into the jungle your path begins to not only wind from side to side, but to go uphill and down as well. You can tell that even now you are beginning to climb up into the foothills of the mountains.

All around you are brilliant green leaves, large and small. Some are split like ferns into hundreds of small arms, and others look like regular leaves, but grown to monster size by the jungle rains and the rich soil. And there are other leaves as well, leaves that are almost black, and some too that are pale yellow and even pink. It feels strange to be surrounded by such unusual plants. After hiking for a few hours, you start to get tired.

Jill: Let's stop here and rest for a bit.

Henry: Yeah, and check the map.

Narrator: "That sounds good to me too," you say.

Jill: OK. Here we are, I think. Wow, we've hiked really far. We're almost half way there!

Henry: Yeah. I think you're right. Aeneas' house is probably only another three or four hours from here. Let's stop again in about an hour and eat lunch.

Jill: Alright.

Narrator: So, you keep going. As the sun rises higher and higher in the sky, the heat gets more intense, and it's very humid among the trees and plants that surround you. Every now and then you see an animal, sometimes big and sometimes very small, moving off the path as you approach. Around the middle of the day you have a tasty lunch, thanks to Claudia, and then you hike on. Around mid afternoon you figure from your map that you're getting close to Aeneas' home. Then quite suddenly you come around a bend in the trail and you see a house built in a clearing, and thousands of banana trees stretching out seemingly endlessly behind it. A man is standing in the front yard of the house. He is holding a big bunch of bananas in one hand, and a big machete or 'cutlass' as Marcus called it, in the other. At first he looks a bit strange and menacing.

Jill: *Salve!*

Aeneas: *Salve.*

Henry: We're looking for a man who lives near here.

Aeneas: Ah. *Loqueris latine?*

Jill: *Non loquor latine. Loquor anglice.* We are trying to learn Latin, though.

Aeneas: I see. Now, *quem quaeritis?*

Henry: Huh?

Aeneas: *Quem quaeritis?* Whom do you seek?

Henry: Oh! Aeneas. We're looking for a man named Aeneas. I think he's supposed to live near here.

Aeneas: Indeed. He does live very near here. In fact, Aeneas and I are *una et eadem*

Continued from Children's Activity Book, page 51

persona—one and the same person. So you may stop looking. Now, what do you want?

Narrator: "Well, Aeneas," you explain, "we need to find a way to get back to the other side of the island, where we came from a couple of days ago, and Claudia said that you might be able to help us."

Aeneas: Ah! You are friends of Claudia! She and I are great friends, although I seldom see her these days.

Henry: Yes, we are friends of Claudia. I'm Henry. And this is Jill.

Narrator: You tell him your name as well. Then you add, "And we love to learn, too, just like all the people here. We're learning Latin as we try to find our way back to the other side of the island. Can you help us?"

Aeneas: Ah! You are learning Latin. That is a wonderful thing indeed. Yes, I might be able to help you…

Narrator: His voice trails off, and you think you see a twinkle come into his eye. Then he says casually:

Aeneas: Of course, for Claudia's sake alone I ought to help you. But how about we make a deal. I'll help the three of you, if you can eat all of these bananas.

Henry: What? Are you serious? There must be fifty of them!

Jill: Yeah, we'll never be able to do it…

Aeneas: Well then, I guess I can do nothing for you!

Henry: Hey, wait, Aeneas. Come on guys. If we have to, we might as well try. Here, give me six to start with.

Aeneas: <laughing> Good attitude, Henry! You are very bold indeed. I like that. However, I meant it only *per jocum*—as a joke. Of course asking you to eat all these bananas at once is unfair. But if you want to learn Latin or any other language, there's a good idea behind my joke. The idea is: DON'T STRESS. Don't worry about how fast you're learning or if you are remembering everything you've learned. If you put too much pressure on yourself, learning becomes a burden, and you actually remember less and don't let yourself guess what things mean. It's works much better to just let the language come to you. Take it one banana at a time, as it were.

Jill: Don't stress! OK. I'm glad it was just a joke, Aeneas. I thought for a minute that you were really going to have us eat all of them!

Aeneas: No, no. But since you are learning Latin, I can tell you a story about a boy every bit as bold as Henry here, a boy who scared off a bear!

Henry: A bear? Wow!

Aeneas: Come inside and share some supper with me while I tell you the story. Then tomorrow we can begin our hike to the high pass. It really is there, if you know where to find it, and we should get you back to your group just in time, since you still have a few days left.

Narrator: "That sounds fantastic," you reply. "Thanks for helping us." Aeneas ushers you all inside his home and in no time you all are comfortably full and reclining in hammocks. Then Aeneas begins to tell you the story of "A Boy and a Bear."

Adventure: The Search for Aeneas

A Boy and a Bear

Although it is important for children to first understand language, it is exciting when they begin to use it, and that is where the learning really takes off. This activity moves in that direction. It is very close in format to the earlier, "A Little Girl and a Mouse" activity.

Instructions for This Page

Have your children look at the first page of the story "A Boy and a Bear" and listen to the introduction to the story on the tape.

Audio Transcript

Narrator 2: Activity: A Boy and a Bear.

Narrator: Here is the story Aeneas tells you. It is called *Puer et Ursus:* A Boy and a Bear.

Match and Learn

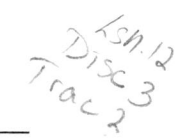

This exercise is visual, audio, and kinesthetic. It is designed to help your children learn by listening and pointing.

Instructions for This Page

Have your children point to the correct boxes and pictures as the tape instructs. In the second part of the exercise, have them answer out loud the questions asked about the numbered pictures.

Have your children pause the tape as needed to have time to give their answers.

Audio Transcript

Narrator: You already know some of these words. Let's go over them. First, point to the *mus*. Did you point to the mouse, in the top white box? Good. Now, point to the *puer*, the boy. The *puer* is in the top gray box, right? Next, point to the bear, the *ursus*. The *ursus* is in the top white box, right? No, the *ursus* is in the bottom gray box. Now, point to the *puella*, the girl. The *puella* is in the bottom white box, right? Good.

Now, see if you can answer some questions about the words you just learned. Look at the picture with the number one next to it.

Number 1. Is this a *puer* or a *mus*? A *mus*? No, this is a *puer*, a boy.

Number 2. Is this an *ursus*? Yes, it is an *ursus*, it is a bear.

Number 3. This is a *puella*, right? No, this is a *mus*, a mouse.

Number 4. This one's an *ursus*, right? No, this one is a *puella*.

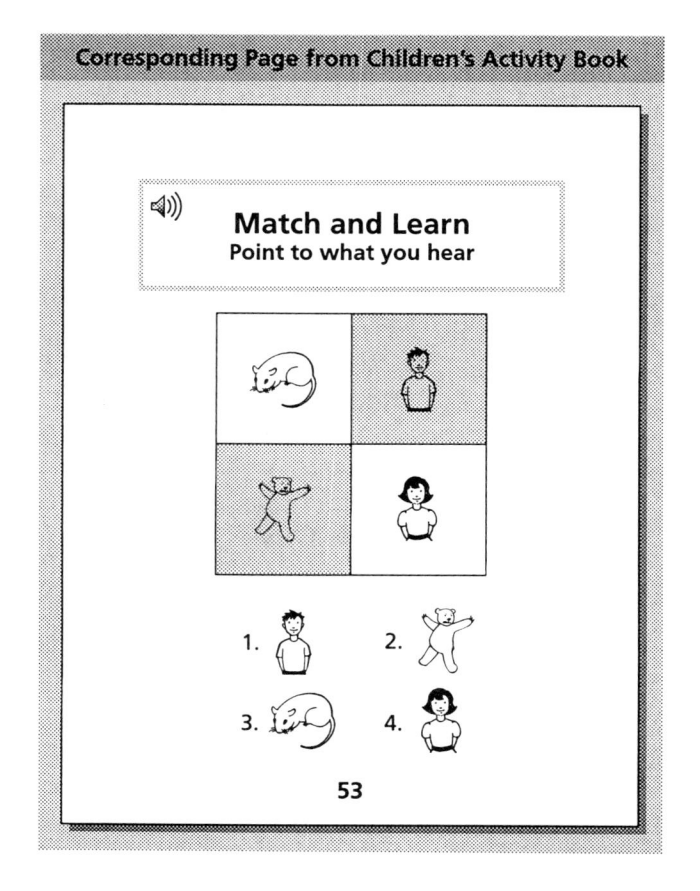

Diglot Weave

This exercise begins a simple bilingual or diglot-weave narrative built around two of the characters from the previous exercises: a boy and a bear. This type of narrative was originally introduced as a language learning aid by Professor Rudy Lentulay of Bryn Mawr University.

Instructions for This Page

Have your children listen carefully and follow the story in their activity books as it is told on the tape.

Have your children follow the words and pictures of the story with their finger, so that when the tape says the Latin word for "bear," for instance, their finger is pointing to the picture of the bear. This kinesthetic connection will enhance their mental connections between the Latin words and the ideas they represent.

Audio Transcript

Narrator: Now listen to Aeneas' story about a boy, a *puer,* and a bear, an *ursus.* Follow along and look at the pictures.

Puer videt ursum. Ursus videt puerum. Ursus roars ferociously: RRR! *Puer* is not afraid. He also roars ferociously: RRR! *Ursus* advances toward *puerum,* roaring: RRR! *Puer* advances toward *ursum,* roaring: RRR! *Ursus* hesitates, then turns back, flees. *Puer* chases *ursum. Ursus,* however, escapes. *Puer* sits down on the ground and laughs. *Ursus* lies down on the ground and cries.

Were you able to follow along? Good. Now, do you remember the word you learned in the story of the girl and the mouse, the word for

---

Corresponding Page from Children's Activity Book

Diglot Weave
Puer et Ursus

👤 videt 🐻. 🐻 videt 👤.
🐻 roars ferociously—RRR!
👤 is not afraid.
He also roars ferociously—RRR!
🐻 advances toward 👤, roaring—RRR!
👤 advances toward 🐻, roaring—RRR!
🐻 hesitates, then turns back, flees.
👤 chases 🐻. 🐻, however, escapes.
👤 🪑 on the ground and 😊.
🐻 🛏 on the ground and 😢.

54

---

sees, *videt;* and the word for chases, *persequitur;* however, *autem;* escapes, *effugit;* and laughs, *ridet?* I hope so, because in this story we'll use some of those same words again!

Match and Learn

This exercise uses frames once again to introduce some new pictures that can then be incorporated into the telling of the story.

Instructions for This Page

Have your children point to the correct pictures as the tape instructs.

Audio Transcript

Narrator: Before I tell this story again, I'll teach you some more words.

Look at frame 1. Point to the box with the boy and the roar sound. This is the top gray box. These two pictures together mean "boy roars." In Latin, "bear roars" is *ursus rugit*. And the Latin word for "roaring" is *rugiens*. That's just *rugit* with a different ending, right? And the different ending makes *rugiens* mean "roaring." And to say "roars ferociously" it's just *rugit ferociter*. Now, point to *puer videt ursum*, "boy sees bear." *Puer videt ursum* is in the top white box, right? Now point to *ursus videt puerum*, "bear sees boy." Did you point to the bottom gray box? Good. Let's keep going.

Look at frame 2. Point to "boy advances toward." This is in the top white box. Do you see it? The big arrow next to the boy means "advances toward." In Latin it's *promovet versus*. Advances toward, *promovet versus*. So the picture in the top white box means *puer promovet versus*, "boy advances toward." Now point to *ursus promovet versus*. It's in the top, gray box, right? Good job. Now point to *puer persequitur ursum*. It is in the bottom gray box, right? Good. Do you remember what *persequitur* means? It means chases. That's right. Now point to "bear hesitates, then turns back." This picture is in the bottom white box. In Latin it is, *ursus dubitat, deinde tergum vertit*. *Ursus* means "bear," of course, and *dubitat* means "hesitates." *Deinde* is Latin for "then," and *vertit* means "he turns back." So, *ursus dubitat, deinde tergum vertit* means, "bear hesitates, then turns back."

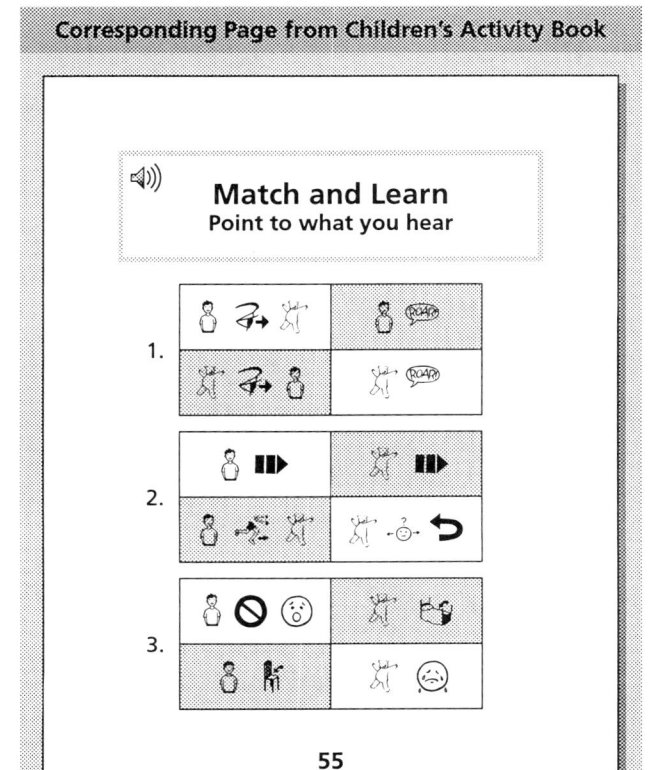

Now look at frame 3. Point to "boy sits on the ground." The arrow pointing to the chair means "sits." In Latin, "he sits on the ground" is *insidit in solo*. So, point to *puer insidit in solo*. It's in the bottom gray box, right? Good job. Now point to "bear lies down on the ground." The arrow pointing to the bed means "lies down." In Latin, "he lies down on the ground" is *jacet in solo*. So, point to *ursus jacet in solo*. It's in the top gray box, right? Now point to "bear cries." The Latin word for "he cries" is *plorat*. Point to *ursus plorat*. Did you point to the bottom white box? Good! Now point to "*puer* is not frightened." It's in the top white box, right? The face with the open mouth means "frightened." In Latin, "the boy is not frightened" is *puer non timet*.

A Boy and a Bear — P–71 — Match and Learn

# Match and Learn

This exercise uses frames once again to introduce a couple more new pictures that can then be incorporated into the telling of the story.

Instructions for This Page

Have your children point to the pictures as directed by the tape.

Have your children pause the tape as needed to have time to give their answers.

Audio Transcript

Narrator: You're doing fine with these new Latin words. Let's learn some more.

Look at frame 4. Do you remember what "he hesitates" is in Latin? That's right, it's *dubitat*. Point to *ursus dubitat*. It's in the bottom gray box, right? Now point to *puer promovet versus ursum*. It's is in the top white box, right? Good. Now point to *puer does not dubitat*. Did you point to the top gray box? Good. Now point to *ursus jacet in solo*. It's in the bottom white box, right?

Now look at frame 5. Point to *ursus plorat*. Did you point to the top gray box? That's right. Now point to *ursus tergum vertit, fugitque*. Did you choose the top white box? Right again! Now point to *puer insidit in solo*. It's is in the bottom gray box, right? Good. Now point to *puer ridet*. Did you point to the bottom white box? Good.

Now look at frame 6. Point to *puer non timet*. Did you point to the bottom white box? Good. Now point to *ursus effugit*, "the bear escapes" or "the bear gets away." This is in the bottom gray box. Now point to *ursus jacet in solo, plorat-que*. It is in the top white box, right? Now point to *puer persequitur ursum*. Did you point to the top gray box? Very well done!

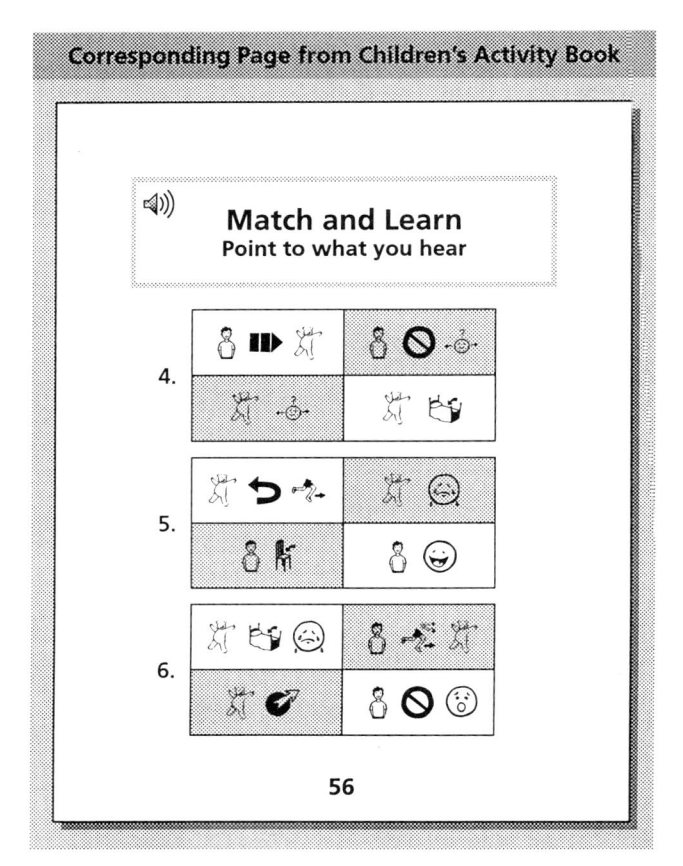

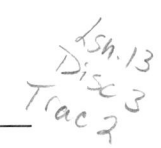

Rebus Story

This exercise is designed to help your children begin to think in Latin. This is accomplished by having pictures in the activity book represent the Latin words read on the tape. This way the children will associate the Latin words with their English equivalents. The Latin words and ideas will be directly associated in their minds.

Instructions for This Page

Have your children follow the pictures with their finger as the Latin words for those pictures are read on the tape.

This is a good exercise for drawing pictures and creating flashcards. Encourage your children to create stories of their own!

Audio Transcript

Narrator: Now that you know the story, try to follow the pictures as I tell you the story all in Latin. Are you ready? Here we go!

Puer videt ursum. Ursus videt puerum. Ursus rugit ferociter: RRR! Puer non timet. Puer etiam rugit ferociter: RRR! Ursus promovet versus puerum, rugiens: RRR! Puer promovet versus ursum, rugiens: RRR! Ursus dubitat, deinde tergum vertit, fugit-que. Puer persequitur ursum. Ursus autem effugit. Puer insidit in solo ridet-que. Ursus jacet in solo, plorat-que.

Were you able to understand the entire story? I hope so. Could you guess what *Puer etiam* meant in the line, *Puer etiam rugit ferociter?* That's right, it means "The boy also." And could you guess what the "*que*" meant on the end of *fugit-que* and *plorat-que?* It means "and." So to say, "The bear lies down on the ground and cries" is *ursus jacet in solo, plorat-que.* That's easy to remember, isn't it?

Corresponding Page from Children's Activity Book

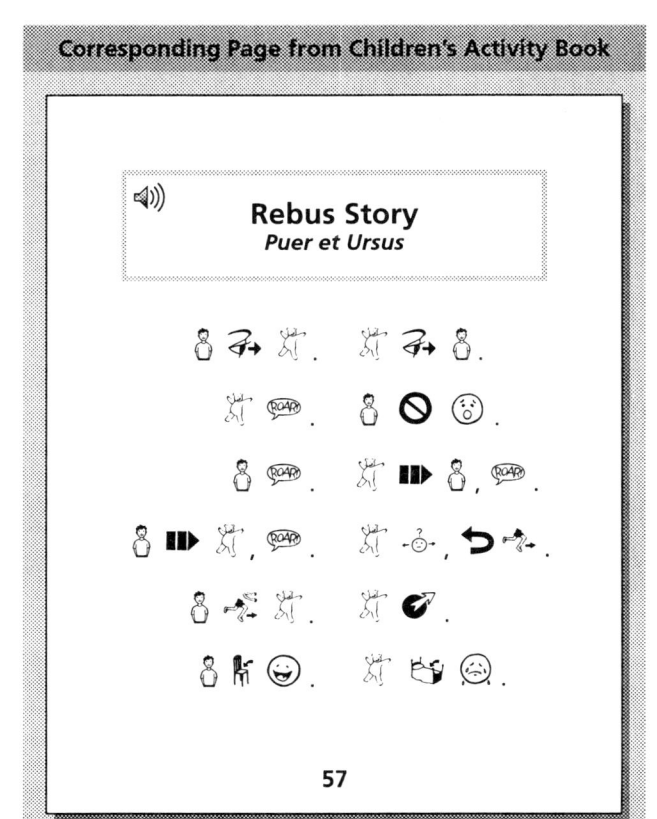

Rebus Story
Puer et Ursus

57

Describe What You See

This exercise requires your children to use the Latin words they learned in the previous exercise to describe the pictures they see.

Instructions for This Page

Have your children say the Latin words for the pictures, or write them on the blank lines to the side of the pictures.

Have your children say or write as many of the Latin words as they can on their own. Then you may go back through with them and help them remember those they missed. Continue to encourage them to guess when they need to, and to not feel bad when they cannot remember all the words or when they get one wrong.

Audio Transcript

Narrator: On this page are some of the pictures you have learned the words for. Say the Latin words for the pictures. Or if you like, write the Latin words for the pictures in the blanks.

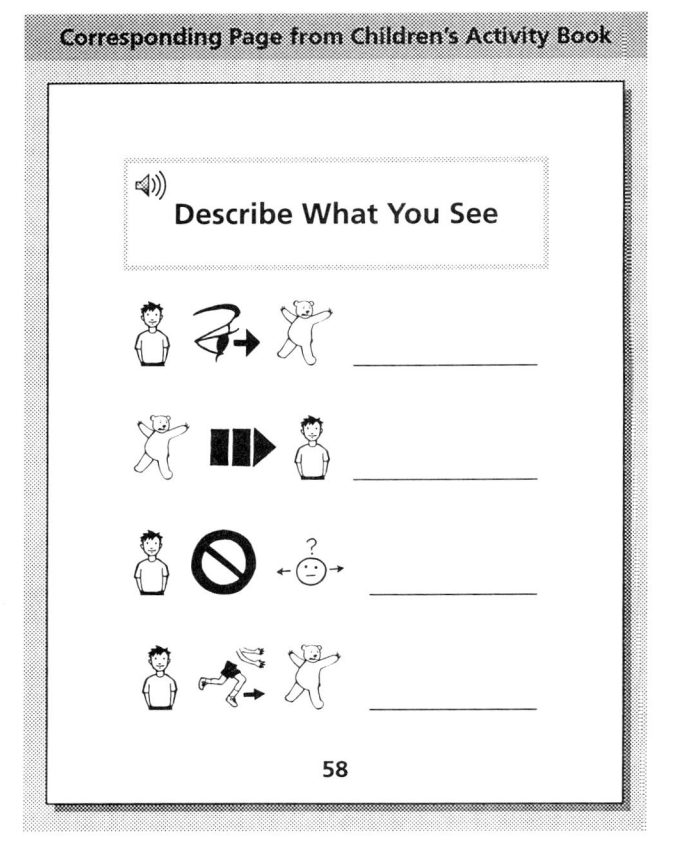

Story Telling

This exercise lets your children use the Latin words they have learned to tell the story of "A Boy and a Bear" themselves.

Instructions for This Page

Have your children follow the trail of pictures (from top to bottom) with their finger, telling the story using the Latin words for the pictured items as they go.

If your children cannot remember a particular word let them think for a moment, and then go ahead and help them. Your goal here is to encourage them to think as hard as they can on their own, while keeping them from getting frustrated or discouraged. Encourage them to create their own stories using the pictures in this exercise.

Audio Transcript

Narrator: Follow the trail of pictures from top to bottom with your finger, telling the story using the Latin words for the pictures.

Corresponding Page from Children's Activity Book

Story Telling
Look at the pictures and tell the story

A Boy and a Bear — P–75 — Story Telling

Practice in Latin

This exercise asks your children to tell the story on their own, using the Latin words they have learned, and using the pictures in the circle as memory prompts.

Instructions for This Page

Have your children look at the pictures in the circle and try to tell the story on their own, using the Latin words they have leaned. Have them record how long it takes them to tell the complete story in Latin their first time, and then their best subsequent time.

Let your children try telling the story as many as six or eight times, each time trying to improve their speed.

Audio Transcript

Narrator: Last of all, use the pictures in the big circle on your activity book page to tell the story again, using the Latin words you have learned. Point to the pictures as you go along, and write down in the first box how long it takes you to tell the story the first time. Then tell the story a few more times, and write down your fastest time in the second box. I'll tell you the story now one more time in Latin, to help you remember all the words.

Puer videt ursum. Ursus videt puerum. Ursus rugit ferociter: RRR! Puer non timet. Hic etiam rugit ferociter: RRR! Ursus promovet versus puerum, rugiens: RRR! Puer promovet versus ursum, rugiens: RRR! Ursus dubitat, deinde tergum vertit, fugit-que. Puer persequitur ursum. Ursus autem effugit. Puer insidit in solo ridet-que. Ursus jacet in solo, plorat-que.

Corresponding Page from Children's Activity Book

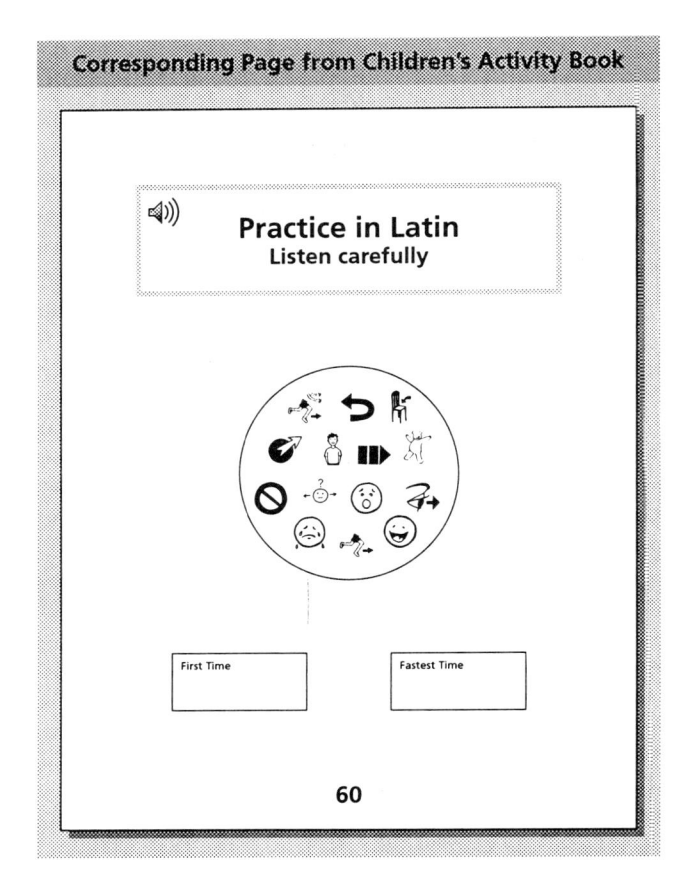

Practice in Latin
Listen carefully

First Time | Fastest Time

60

Now you tell the story and record your times.

Were you able to tell the story on your own? Good. What was your fastest time?

A Boy and a Bear — P–76 — Practice in Latin

To the Waterfall!

This section contains an audio transcript of the adventure story your children will hear on the tape.

Instructions for This Page

Have your children listen carefully as the adventure story is read on the tape. Encourage your children to take an active part in listening to the adventure story. Ask them to respond to things they hear and have them say out loud words said by the characters on the tape.

Younger children might enjoy coloring the picture as the adventure story is read. Older children may want to follow along with the written audio transcript provided in this *Parent's Guide*.

Audio Transcript

Narrator 2: The Adventure Continues: To the Waterfall!

Narrator: The next morning you set out with Jill, Henry and your new guide, Aeneas, to find the high mountain pass in the middle of the island that will take you back to your tour group. The jungle is so much more fascinating and less forbidding with Aeneas along telling you the Latin names of all the wild beasts—the *ferae bestiae,* and plants, and pointing out dozens of things you hadn't noticed before.

Jill: Thanks for teaching us Latin words for things, Aeneas. It makes the jungle seem so much friendlier to know what all the plants and animals are called.

Corresponding Page from Children's Activity Book

The Adventure Continues
To the Waterfall!

61

Henry: Yeah, and it's cool to learn their names in Latin because they're the same names scientists have been using for hundreds of years.

Aeneas: That's true, Henry. And before that the Romans and others used the names.

Narrator: You think about the jungle around you and about the Roman Empire that flourished two thousand years ago as you hike through the jungle. All around you now you recognize plants that Aeneas has taught you the names for, and you feel like you're walking through history. As you walk, Aeneas tells you more about the Latin language and the people who have spoken and written it down through history.

Henry: That's really interesting, Aeneas. I always thought Latin would be a cool language to know, because of all the old Roman ruins I've seen pictures of, but I never thought I'd actually get to learn it. It just seemed so old, almost like something people had forgotten about.

Continued from Children's Activity Book, page 61

Aeneas: Not all people, Henry. We use it here on our side of the island, of course, but even where you live and in many other places Latin is a valuable language to know. You see, several languages people still speak today came down from Latin, languages like French and Spanish, Italian and Portuguese and Romanian—and other languages you have probably never heard of. Learning Latin gives you a great foundation to build on in learning other languages. You may not know it, but thousands and thousands of words in English come from Latin, too. You see, Latin is really a treasure chest of a language.

Jill: That's just what Marcus told us!

Aeneas: Oh, did he? Good! It's good to know that our children appreciate the rich heritage we have from the Latin language.

Narrator: You, Jill and Henry all listen carefully as Aeneas talks, and you hardly notice the passing of time. As you walk along you feel the cool morning air becoming warmer as the sun rises higher and higher in the sky above you. After a simple lunch, you all find comfortable beds in the lush grasses and moss by the side of the path, and rest for a couple of hours. The entire jungle seems to rest with you, for with the sun shining down so intensely on the treetops, even in the shade of the trees there is a drowsy feeling over everything. When it's time to get moving again, Aeneas says:

Aeneas: Well, that felt good to rest for a bit, eh?

Jill: Yeah. I feel ready for more hiking now. And I think I can even hear some wind blowing through the leaves of the trees up above us.

Henry: I heard that sound too, but it was just before I fell asleep. What is it, Aeneas?

Aeneas: You children must have good ears. I believe you are hearing the sound of a great waterfall that is on our trail, but still a good way ahead. We should be there in half an hour. The waterfall marks the real beginning of the mountains.

Henry: All right! We're making good progress, then!

Aeneas: Yes, indeed. You are all good hikers. We should reach the top of the falls in time to make our camp tonight, and then tomorrow I hope to make it all the way to the home of Antonia, who lives very near to the pass you seek.

Jill: Antonia? Who is she?

Aeneas: She is a weaver. She weaves beautiful blankets and tapestries. She was a great friend of my mother's, years ago. She is very old, and very wise and gracious. We will stay with her tomorrow night, and return you through the pass to your friends the next day, if all goes well.

Henry: That sounds like a good plan to me!

Narrator: So you continue your journey. Every minute, so it seems, the sound of the distant waterfall gets louder.

Henry: Wow! It sounds like we're practically right under the waterfall now, but I still can't see it yet!

Narrator: "Yeah," you agree, "It must be huge to make so much noise. The roar of the falling water sounds like a big airplane taking off."

Aeneas: Yes. It is indeed a great waterfall. Certainly it is the tallest on the island. It falls more than two hundred feet, and the pool at its base is very deep. Ah, look, now you can begin to see it through the trees!

Narrator: Immediately ahead of you now, you see towering cliffs, black in the afternoon sun, with tons of rushing white water spilling over the cliff tops and gushing down, down, into a huge spreading pool, emerald green and seemingly bottomless. The pool's edge ends just twenty yards in front of you. Here at the base of the falls the sound of the falling water

Adventure: To the Waterfall!

Continued from Children's Activity Book, page 61

is almost deafening. You call out to Jill and Henry: "Wow, look how tall it is!"

Henry: Yeah, how are we ever going to get to the top of it, Aeneas?

Narrator: Aeneas doesn't say anything, he just points around the pool to your left, where you now notice that the trail leads. Moving his pointing finger back and forth in a long series of z's, Aeneas traces the outline of your path upward along the cliff face to the side of the waterfall.

Jill: No way! You've got to be joking again, Aeneas. There is no way we can make it up that zigzag-y path. It goes right up the face of the cliffs!

Henry: And they're really tall, and the rock looks slick!

Aeneas: It is a dangerous climb, and we will need to be very careful and stay as far back from the edge as we can. The path is actually wider than it looks from here, and there are ropes and chains fastened to the rocks in some particularly treacherous places. We can hold on to those, and we should get up all right. But first let's go back into the shade of the trees and rest up a bit for the climb. While we rest I'll tell you another story in Latin!

A Hungry Giant

It is important for children to first understand spoken language, but it is more exciting when they begin to use it, and that is where the learning really takes off. In this activity we continue with comprehension building, but as the exercises progress, we gradually introduce conversation.

Your children will hear a story about a hungry giant several times. They will learn the character names and identify them with pictures. By the time we get to their telling the story, they will have learned to recognize the pictures well enough that they can pretty much tell the story simply by looking at the pictures.

This story is more challenging than the previous story, "A Boy and a Bear," and the discussion of the story on the tape uses more Latin.

Corresponding Page from Children's Activity Book

A Hungry Giant
Fabula

Instructions for This Page

Have your children look at the first page of the story "A Hungry Giant" and listen to the introduction to the story on the tape.

Audio Transcript

Narrator 2: Activity: A Hungry Giant.

Narrator: As you rest at the base of the waterfall, Aeneas offers to tell you a story, and teach you some new Latin words at the same time. He calls his story "A Hungry Giant."

Power-Glide **Children's Latin**

Match and Learn

This exercise is visual, audio, and kinesthetic. It is designed to help your children learn by listening and pointing.

Instructions for This Page

Have your children point to the correct boxes and pictures as the tape instructs. In the second part of the exercise have them answer out loud the questions asked about the numbered pictures. The purpose of this exercise is simply to teach the system of frames and numbered pictures in preparation for Latin learning using these tools in subsequent sections.

Have your children pause the tape as needed to have time to give their answers.

Corresponding Page from Children's Activity Book

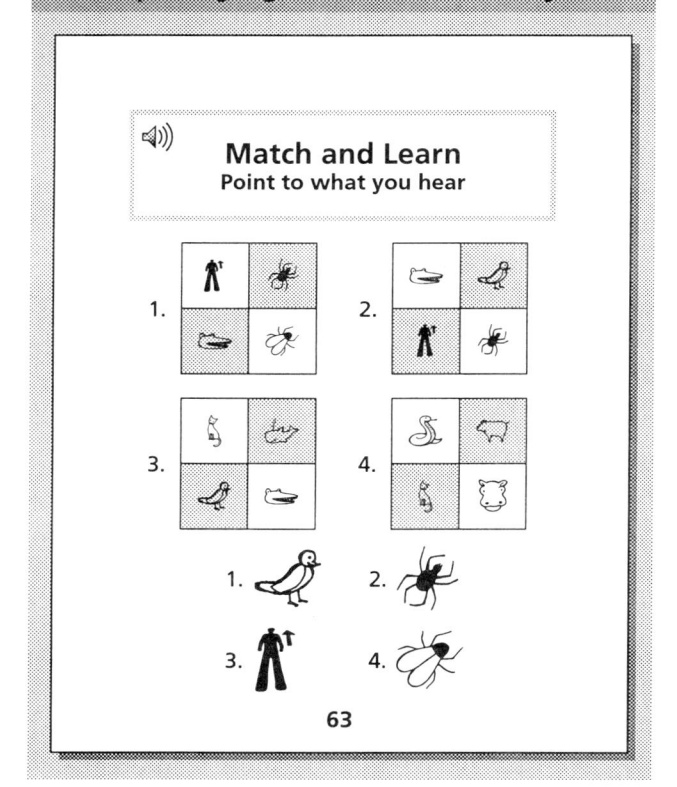

Match and Learn
Point to what you hear

Audio Transcript

Narrator: Before I tell you this *fabula*, I'll teach you some new words to help you understand.

Look at frame 1. Point to the giant, the *gigas*. The *gigas* is in the top white box, right? Now point to the crocodile, the *crocodilus*. The *crocodilus* is in the bottom gray box, right? Now point to the fly, the *musca*. Is the *musca* in the top gray box? No, the *musca* is in the bottom white box, right? Now point to the spider, the *arena*. It is in the top gray box, right?

Now look at frame 2. Point to the *arena*. It is in the bottom white box, right? Now point to the *crocodilus*. He is in the top white box, right? Now point to the *gigas*. It is in the bottom gray box, right? Now point to the *avis*, the bird. It is in the top gray box, right?

Now look at frame 3. Point to the *avis*. It is in the top gray box, right? No, the *avis* is in the bottom gray box. Now point to the whale, the *balaena*. It is in the top gray box, right? Now point to the *feles*, the cat. It is in the top white box, right? Yes. Now point to the *crocodilus*. It is in the bottom gray box, right? No, it is in the bottom white box.

Now look at frame 4. Point to the hippopotamus, the *hippopotamus*. The *hippopotamus* is in the bottom white box, right? Yes. Now point to the *porcus*, the pig. The *porcus* is in the top gray box, right? Now point to the *serpens*, the snake. The *serpens* is in the bottom gray box, right? No, the *serpens* is in the top white box. Now point to the *feles*. The *feles* is in the bottom gray box, right?

Now see if you can answer some questions about the words you just learned. Look at the picture with the number one next to it.

Number 1. Is this an *avis*? Yes, this is an *avis*.

Number 2. Is this an *arena*? Yes, this is an *arena*.

Number 3. Is this a *gigas* or a *musca*? Did you say a giant, a *gigas*? Yes, this is a *gigas*.

Number 4. Is this an *arena*? No, this is a *musca*.

A Hungry Giant — Match and Learn

Match and Learn

This exercise uses frames once again to introduce some new pictures and Latin words that can then be incorporated into the telling of the story.

Instructions for This Page

Have your children point to the correct pictures as the tape instructs. In the second half of the exercise have them answer out loud the questions asked about the numbered pictures.

💡 As these activities become progressively more challenging, the main objective is to help your children feel confident. They should not be overly concerned with correctness. Encourage them to point boldly as soon as they hear what to point to in the first half of the exercise, and to speak out loud in response to the questions in the second half. When your children guess wrong, let them know it's okay and to keep making their best guesses.

Audio Transcript

🔊 Narrator: Did you do well with those pictures and words? Good. Let's try a few more.

Look at frame 5. Point to the *leopardus*. The *leopardus*, the leopard, is in the top gray box, right? Now point to the *gigas*. The *gigas* is in the bottom white box, right? No, it is in the bottom gray box. Now point to the *musca*. The *musca* is in the bottom white box, right? Yes. Now point to the *crocodilus*. It's in the top white box, right? Yes!

Now look at frame 6. Point to the *leopardus et* the *musca*. They are in the top gray box, right? Yes. Now point to the *crocodilus et* the *balaena*. They are in the bottom gray box, right? No, they are in the top white box. Point to the *avis et* the *crocodilus*. The *avis et* the *crocodilus* are in the bottom gray box, right? Yes. Now point to the *serpens* and the *porcus*. The *serpens et* the *porcus* are in the bottom white box, right?

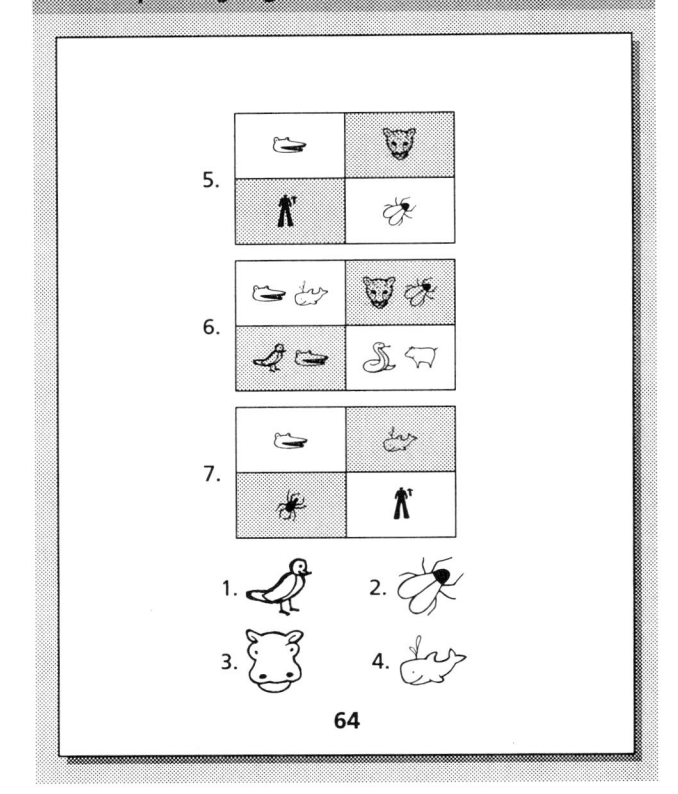

Now look at frame 7. Point to the *gigas*. The *gigas* is in the bottom white box, right? Yes. Now point to the *balaena*. It is in the top gray box, right? Yes. Now point to the *arena*. It is in the bottom white box? No, it is in the bottom gray box. Now point to the *crocodilus*. It's in the top white box, right? Yes.

Now, see if you can answer some questions about the words you just learned.

Look at picture 1. Is this an *avis*? Yes, this is an *avis*.

Picture number 2. Is this a *crocodilus* or a *musca*? It is a *musca*.

Picture number 3. Is this a *balaena*? No, this is a *hippopotamus*.

Picture number 4 is *a crocodilus*, right? No, it is a *balaena*.

A Hungry Giant — Match and Learn

Power-Glide **Children's Latin**

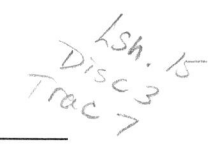

Match and Learn

This exercise uses frames once again to introduce some new pictures that can then be incorporated into the telling of the story.

Instructions for This Page

Have your children point to the correct pictures as the tape instructs. Have your children pause the tape as needed to have time to give their answers.

> Have your children come up with frames of their own! These can then be used as flashcards.

Audio Transcript

Narrator: Here are a few more pictures and new words to learn.

Look at frame 1. Point to the *serpens*. It is in the top white box, right? Yes. Now point to *crocodilus edit arenam*, the crocodile ate the spider. It is in the bottom gray box, right? Yes. Now point to *balaena edit crocodilum*. Is "the whale ate the crocodile" in the bottom white box? Yes, it is. Now point to the *leopardus*. The *leopardus* is in the top gray box, right? Yes.

Now look at frame 2. Point to *vir cogitavit,* the man thought. *Vir cogitavit* is in the top white box, right? Yes. Now point to the *feles cogitavit*. Can you guess what this means? That's right! It means, "The cat thought." It's in the bottom gray box, right? Yes. Now point to *crocodilus edit avem.* That's in the bottom white box, right? Now point to *balaena cogitavit*. That is in the bottom gray box, right? No, it is in the top gray box.

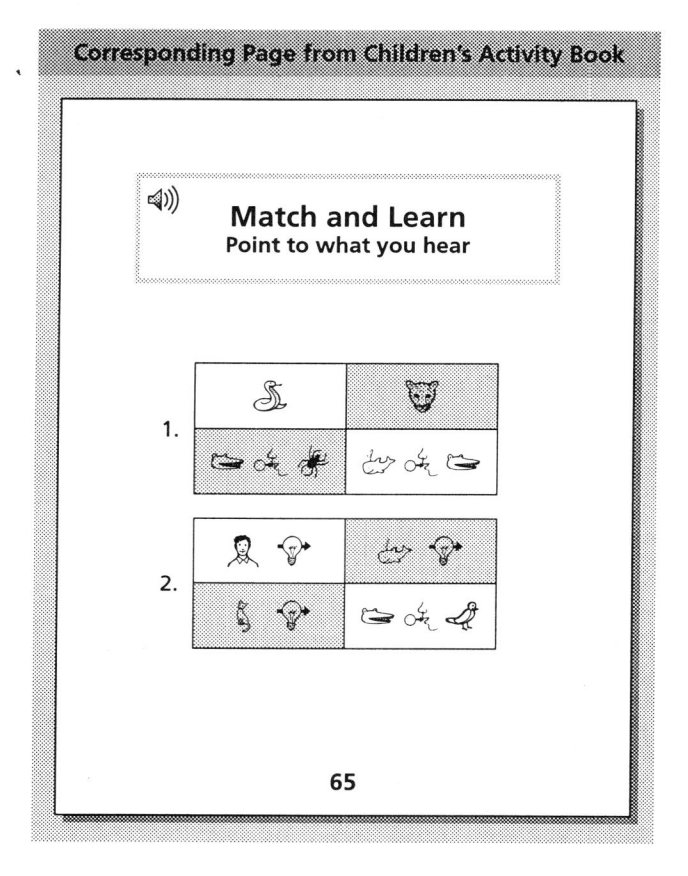

Corresponding Page from Children's Activity Book

Match and Learn
Point to what you hear

1.
2.

A Hungry Giant — Match and Learn

Describe What You See

This exercise requires your children to use the Latin words they learned in the previous exercises to describe the pictures they see.

Instructions for This Page

Have your children say the Latin words for the pictures, or write them on the blank lines to the side of the pictures.

Have your children say or write as many of the Latin words as they can on their own. Then you may go back through with them and help them remember those they missed. Continue to encourage them to guess when they need to, and to not feel bad when they cannot remember all the words or when they get one wrong.

Audio Transcript

Narrator: On this page are some of the pictures you have learned the words for. Say the Latin words for the pictures. Or if you like, write the Latin words for the pictures in the blanks.

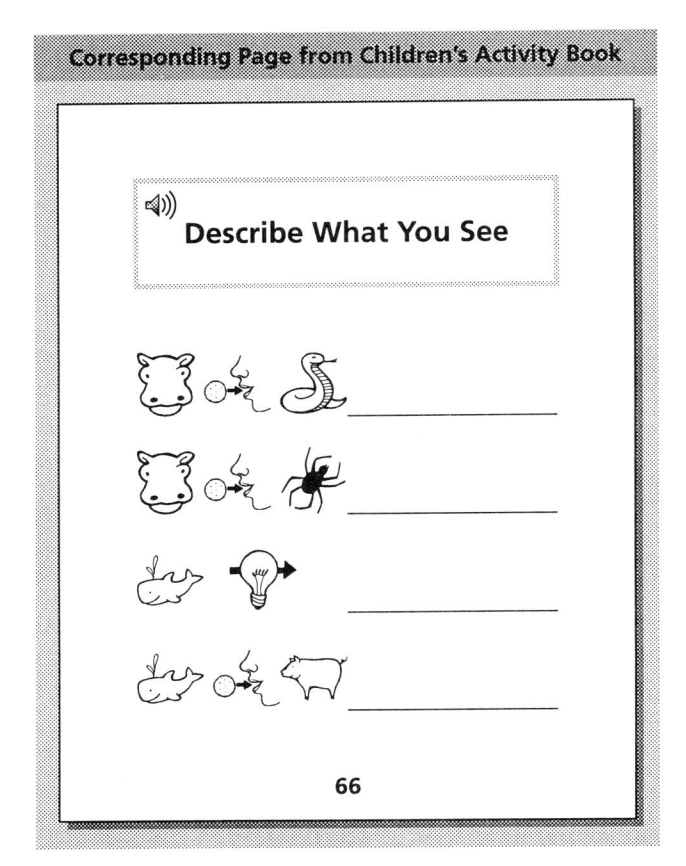

A Hungry Giant — Describe What You See

Diglot Weave

The following multi-page exercise contains an extended diglot-weave narrative built around the words from the previous exercises.

Instructions for This Page

Have your children listen carefully and follow the story in their activity books as it is told on the tape. In this story, English words that don't really need to be included (because their meaning is already included in the Latin words) are in small plain font.

Have your children follow the words and pictures of the story with their finger, so that when the tape says the Latin word for "giant," for instance, their finger points to the picture of the giant. This kinesthetic connection will enhance their mental connections between the Latin words and the ideas they represent.

If the pace is ever too fast, stop the tape and review with your children. Be sure to reward understanding and encourage listening. The exercise is designed to help your children develop comprehension of main ideas. You may wish to point to the pictures and have them give the Latin equivalents. Keep in mind, however, that comprehension of every word is not nearly as important as overall comprehension—understanding the main ideas of the story.

Audio Transcript

Narrator: Now listen to the story of "A Hungry Giant." Follow along and look at the pictures.

Have you ever seen a *gigantem*? Do you know how big a *gigas* is? Do you know how much a *gigas* can eat? I haven't ever *vidi* a *gigantem*, but one time my father (*pater meus*) saw one. Anyway *pater meus* told me he saw a *gigantem*. This happened *cum* he was a *puer* your age.

Corresponding Page from Children's Activity Book

Diglot Weave
A Hungry Giant

Have you ever seen a *gigantem*? Do you know how big a *gigas* is? Do you know how much a *gigas* can eat? I haven't ever *vidi* a *gigantem*, but one time my father (*pater meus*) saw one. Anyway *pater meus* told me he saw a *gigantem*. This happened *cum* he was a *puer* your age.

67

Diglot Weave

This is the next section of the multi-page diglot-weave narrative of "A Hungry Giant."

Instructions for This Page

Have your children continue to listen carefully and follow the story in their activity books as it is told on the tape.

Audio Transcript

Narrator: One morning before breakfast he was taking a walk. While he *ambularet*, he *vidit* a *muscam*. The *musca* was caught in a spider's web. He watched the *arenam* come and eat the *muscam*.

"*Optime!*" ("Good!") *cogitavit pater meus.* "*Arena muscam edit.* I don't like flies. . . . *Non placent mihi muscae.*"

Corresponding Page from Children's Activity Book

One morning before breakfast he was taking a walk. While he *ambularet*, he *vidit* a *muscam*. The *musca* was caught in a spider's web. He watched the *arenam* come and eat the *muscam*.

"*Optime!*" ("Good!") *cogitavit pater meus.* "*Arena muscam edit.* I don't like flies. . . . *Non placent mihi muscae.*"

68

Diglot Weave

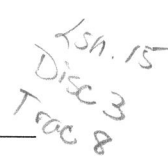

This is the next section of the multi-page diglot-weave narrative of "A Hungry Giant."

Instructions for This Page

Have your children continue to listen carefully and follow the story in their activity books as it is told on the tape.

Audio Transcript

Narrator: A moment later, an *avis* came up (*advenit*) et arenam edit. "*Optime,*" cogitavit pater meus. "*Avis arenam edit. Non placent mihi arenae.*"

But after a bit, a *feles advenit et avem edit. Et pater meus cogitavit:* "It's sad, *triste est, feles avem edit.* I like birds. . . . *Aves placent mihi.*"

Corresponding Page from Children's Activity Book

A moment later, an *avis* came up (*advenit*) et arenam edit. "*Optime,*" cogitavit pater meus. "*Avis arenam edit. Non placent mihi arenae.*"

But after a bit, a *feles advenit et avem edit. Et pater meus cogitavit:* "It's sad, *triste est,* that the *feles avem edit.* I like birds. . . . *Aves placent mihi.*"

69

Diglot Weave

This is the next section of the multi-page diglot-weave narrative of "A Hungry Giant."

Instructions for This Page

Have your children continue to listen carefully and follow the story in their activity books as it is told on the tape.

Audio Transcript

Narrator: But after that, *serpens advenit et felem edit. Et pater meus cogitavit: "Triste est, feles placent mihi."*

But after a bit, *advenit porcus et serpentem edit. Et pater meus cogitavit: "Optime, porcus serpentem edit. Non placent mihi serpentes."*

Corresponding Page from Children's Activity Book

But after that, *a serpens advenit et felem edit. Et pater meus cogitavit: "Triste est, feles placent mihi."*

But after a bit, *advenit porcus et serpentem edit. Et pater meus cogitavit: "Optime, porcus serpentem edit. Non placent mihi serpentes."*

Diglot Weave

This is the next section of the multi-page diglot-weave narrative of "A Hungry Giant."

Instructions for This Page

Have your children continue to listen carefully and follow the story in their activity books as it is told on the tape.

Audio Transcript

Narrator: Before long, *advenit leopardus et porcum edit. Et pater meus cogitavit:* "Wow, *leopardus porcum edit.* Such excitement! – *Talis commotionem!*"

A while later, *advenit crocodilus et leopardum edit. Et pater meus cogitavit:* "Wow, *crocodilus leopardum edit. Talis commotionem!* What will happen now? – *Quid accidet nunc?*"

Corresponding Page from Children's Activity Book

Before long, *advenit leopardus et porcum edit. Et pater meus cogitavit:* "Wow, *leopardus porcum edit.* Such excitement! – *Talis commotionem!*"

A while later, *advenit crocodilus et leopardum edit. Et pater meus cogitavit:* "Wow, *crocodilus leopardum edit. Talis commotionem!* What will happen now? – *Quid accidet nunc?*"

71

Diglot Weave

This is the next section of the multi-page diglot-weave narrative of "A Hungry Giant."

Instructions for This Page

Have your children continue to listen carefully and follow the story in their activity books as it is told on the tape.

Audio Transcript

Narrator: Before long, *advenit hippopotamus et crocodilum edit. Et pater meus cogitavit:* "Oh my, *hippopotamus crocodilum edit! Quid accidet nunc?*"

A moment later, *advenit balaena et hippopotamum edit. Et pater meus cogitavit:* "Wow, this is too much—*hoc est nimium!*

Corresponding Page from Children's Activity Book

Before long, *advenit hippopotamus et crocodilum edit. Et pater meus cogitavit:* "Oh my, *hippopotamus crocodilum edit! Quid accidet nunc?*"

A moment later, *advenit balaena et hippopotamum edit. Et pater meus cogitavit:* "Wow, this is too much—*hoc est nimium!*

72

Diglot Weave

This is the next section of the multi-page diglot-weave narrative of "A Hungry Giant."

Instructions for This Page

Have your children continue to listen carefully and follow the story in their activity books as it is told on the tape.

Audio Transcript

Narrator: Just imagine: *Balaena hippopotamum edit, hippopotamus crocodilum edit, crocodilus leopardum edit, leopardus porcum edit, porcus serpentem edit, serpens felem edit, feles avem edit, avis arenam edit, et arena muscam edit!* That's amazing! I've never seen—*numquam vidi*—such a thing."

Corresponding Page from Children's Activity Book

Just imagine:

Balaena hippopotamum edit, hippopotamus crocodilum edit, crocodilus leopardum edit, leopardus porcum edit, porcus serpentem edit, serpens felem edit, feles avem edit, avis arenam edit, et arena muscam edit!

That's amazing! I've never seen—*numquam vidi*—such a thing."

Diglot Weave

This is the next section of the multi-page diglot-weave narrative of "A Hungry Giant."

Instructions for This Page

Have your children continue to listen carefully and follow the story in their activity books as it is told on the tape.

Audio Transcript

Narrator: Suddenly a *manus* reached down from the sky *et* picked up *balaenam*. *Pater meus* looked up just as the *gigas* swallowed it whole. *Et cogitavit:* "Wow, this is the first time I've *gigantem vidi*.

Maybe he's still hungry. I'd better get out of here!" And he *cucurrit* home as fast as he could.

Corresponding Page from Children's Activity Book

Suddenly a *manus* reached down from the sky *et* picked up *balaenam*. *Pater meus* looked up just as the *gigas* swallowed it whole. *Et* he *cogitavit:* "Wow, this is the first time I've *gigantem vidi*.

Maybe he's still hungry. I'd better get out of here!" And he *cucurrit* home as fast as he could.

74

Power-Glide **Children's Latin**

Diglot Weave

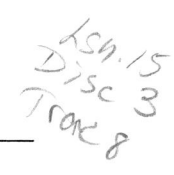

This is the last section of the multi-page diglot-weave narrative about "A Hungry Giant."

Instructions for This Page

Have your children continue to listen carefully and follow the story in their activity books as it is told on the tape.

Audio Transcript

🔊 Narrator: And there, as he ate a big bowl of mush, *he cogitavit* of the *muscā, et arenā et avi, et fele et serpente, et porco et leopardo, et crocodilo et hippopotamo, et balaenā.*

But most of all *he cogitavit* of the *gigante, et* how hungry, how *esuriens*, he must have been.

Corresponding Page from Children's Activity Book

And there, as he ate a big bowl of mush, He *cogitavit* of the *muscā, et arenā et avi, et fele et serpente, et porco et leopardo, et crocodilo et hippopotamo, et balaenā.*

But most of all he *cogitavit* of the *gigante, et* how hungry, how *esuriens*, he must have been.

A Hungry Giant — Diglot Weave

Story Telling

This exercise lets your children use the Latin words they have learned to tell the story of "A Hungry Giant" themselves.

Instructions for This Page

Have your children follow the trail of pictures (from top to bottom) with their finger, telling the story using the Latin words for the pictured items as they go. The diagonal lines separate sections of the story.

If your children cannot remember a particular word let them think for a moment, and then go ahead and help them. Your goal here is to encourage them to think as hard as they can on their own, while keeping them from getting discouraged. Encourage them to create their own stories if they like, using the pictures in this exercise.

You'll notice that a few pictographs, namely "laughs," "cries," "hand," and "runs" are used in this section, but were not introduced in the beginning of "Hungry Giant." Your children should have learned these pictographs from "A Boy and a Bear" and "Body Parts." See if your children can remember them as they proceed through this activity.

Audio Transcript

Narrator: Now it's your turn to tell the story. Follow the trail of pictures from top to bottom with your finger, telling the story using as many Latin words as you can. The pictures will remind you how the story goes, and don't worry when you have to put in some English.

A Hungry Giant

Story Telling

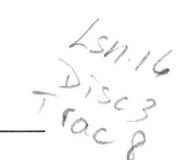

This exercise lets your children use the Latin words they have learned to tell the story of "A Hungry Giant" themselves.

Instructions for This Page

Have your children follow the trail of pictures (from top to bottom) with their finger, telling the story using the Latin words for the pictured items as they go.

If your children cannot remember a particular word let them think for a moment, and then go ahead and help them. Your goal here is to encourage them to think as much as they can on their own, while keeping them from getting discouraged. Encourage them to create their own stories using the pictures in this exercise.

Corresponding Page from Children's Activity Book

Story Telling
Look at the pictures and tell the story

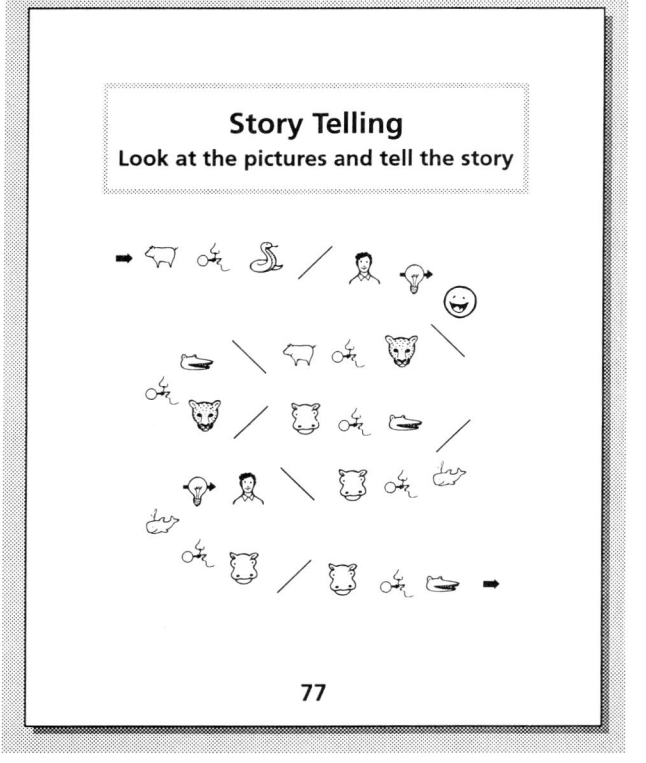

A Hungry Giant

Story Telling

This exercise lets your children use the Latin words they have learned to tell the story of "A Hungry Giant" themselves.

Instructions for This Page

Have your children follow the trail of pictures (from top to bottom) with their finger, telling the story using the Latin words for the pictured items as they go.

If your children cannot remember a particular word let them think for a moment, and then go ahead and help them. Your goal here is to encourage them to think as hard as they can on their own, while keeping them from getting frustrated or discouraged. Encourage them to create their own stories using the pictures in this exercise.

Practice in Latin

This exercise asks your children to tell the story of "A Hungry Giant" themselves using the pictures from the story as memory prompts.

Instructions for This Page

Have your children point to the pictures in the circle in their activity books as they tell the story of "A Hungry Giant" on their own, using the Latin words they have learned. Record how long it takes them to tell the complete story in Latin their first time, and then record their best time on a third or fourth attempt.

If necessary, review the story with your children, using the audio transcript provided in this *Parent's Guide*.

Audio Transcript

Narrator: Now that you have reviewed the story, see how much of it you can tell by yourself. All the pictures used in the story are in the big circle on your activity book page. Point to the pictures in the right order as you tell the story. Turn the tape off as you tell the story, and turn it on again when you finish.

Were you able to tell the whole story on your own, with mostly Latin words? Excellent!

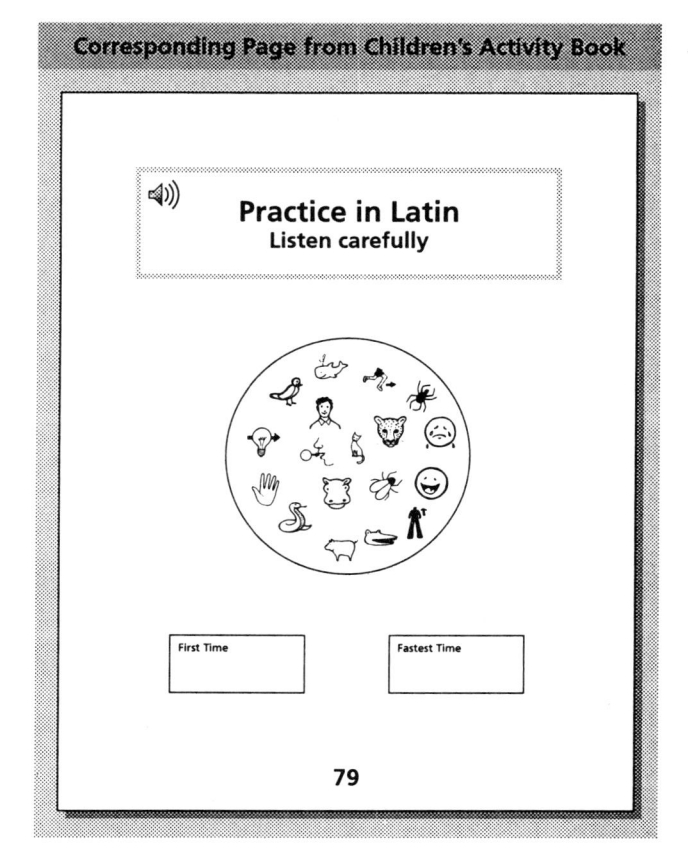

Corresponding Page from Children's Activity Book

Practice in Latin
Listen carefully

First Time   Fastest Time

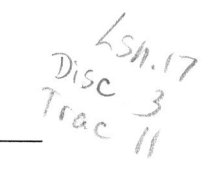

Cliff Climbing and Jungle Camp

This section contains an audio transcript of the adventure story your children will hear on the tape.

Instructions for This Page

Have your children listen carefully as the adventure story is read on the tape.

Encourage your children to take an active part in listening to the adventure story. Ask them to respond to things they hear and have them say out loud words said by the characters on the tape. Younger children might enjoy coloring the picture as the adventure story is read. Older children may want to follow along with the written audio transcript provided in this *Parent's Guide*.

Audio Transcript

Narrator 2: The Adventure Continues: Cliff Climbing and Jungle Camp

Aeneas: Well, did you enjoy my story?

Jill: Yes, very much!

Henry: Yeah!

Aeneas: Good! Now we really had better get going again. The only thing that would not do at all would be to get caught on the cliff face in the dark, so, *est periculum in morā*—there is danger in delay. Let's go on then! Or, as we say in Latin, *pro cedamus!*

Henry: *Pro cedamus!*

Narrator: "Yeah, *pro cedamus!*" you agree. And with that you begin the most dangerous part of your hike, right up the steep cliff face, as the afternoon suns shines down through the mist that rises high above the falls. The rocky trail is slippery, just as Henry warned, and you make your way up very carefully, step by step. At last you reach the top, and turning around, look back down the way you have come.

Jill: Hey you guys, look! You can see clear to the ocean from up here!

Narrator: "Yeah," you add. "And look down at the pool where we were an hour ago. It looks like a little pond, with miniature trees next to it. We've come up really high."

Henry: Yeah we have. We can see for miles and miles up here, I bet.

Aeneas: This view is quite breathtaking. I've often thought of moving up here, but bananas grow much better down below, and I could never carry much down the cliffs to sell. Well, let's hike in a bit from the edge of the cliff and make our camp. There is a perfect little wooded hollow not far from here where we'll be quite comfortable.

Continued from Children's Activity Book, page 81

Narrator: You hike inland from the cliffs for another five minutes or so, and reach the camping spot Aeneas has chosen. Soon you have your beds laid out on soft moss, and a campfire crackling cheerfully as dusk sets in. After a hearty supper you relax around the fire and Aeneas says:

Aeneas: Well, so long as we have such a pleasant campfire to sit around, I think I'll tell you another story.

Jill: That would be great!

Henry: Yeah!

Diglot Weave

This activity is a full-fledged diglot-weave story, which means that, unlike the diglot-weave/rebus stories encountered so far, it uses no pictures to tell the story. The actual Latin words are used instead.

This story is taken directly from Power-Glide's adult Latin course, and is intended as a preparation for that course. In order to prepare your children to follow the plot of the story, all new words used in the story are taught through Match and Learn activities before the story begins.

Instructions for This Page

Have your children look at the picture in their activity book and listen to the introduction to the story of "The Broken Window."

Audio Transcript

Narrator 2: Activity: Diglot-Weave Story. The Broken Window.

Narrator: As you all sit around the campfire, Aeneas offers to tell you a story and teach you some more Latin at the same time. You eagerly agree and he begins his story, a story called "The Broken Window."

Match and Learn

This exercise uses Match and Learn frames to introduce some new words that will be used in the story.

Instructions for This Page

Have your children look at the frames in their activity book and point to the pictures as the tape directs them. Have your children pause the tape as needed to have time to give their answers.

Audio Transcript

Narrator: Before I tell you Aeneas' story, let me teach you a few new words so you can follow along. Look at the frames in your activity book and point to what you hear. Are you ready?

OK, here we go!

Look at frame 1. Point to the *lupus*, the wolf. It's in the top white box, right? Now point to the *canis*. It's in the bottom gray box, right? Now point to the *femina*. The *femina* is in the bottom white box, right? Now point to the *vir*, the man. He is in the top gray box. Did you point to them all? Good job.

Now look at frame 2. Point to the *puella*. The girl is in the bottom gray box, right? Now point to the *puer*. He is in the top white box, right? Now point to the group of three children. Can you guess what a group of children is called in Latin? They are called *liberi*. Point to the *liberi* in the top gray box. Now point to the last picture in this frame. What is it a picture of? A *canis*? That's right!

Now look at frame 3. Point to the *nasus*. Did you remember that *nasus* is the word for nose? Good! Now point to the *domus*. *Domus* is the Latin word for house. Now point to the *fenestra*. A *fenestra* is a window. Did you guess right? Good! Now point to the door. The Latin word for door is *janua*. Say it out loud: *janua*.

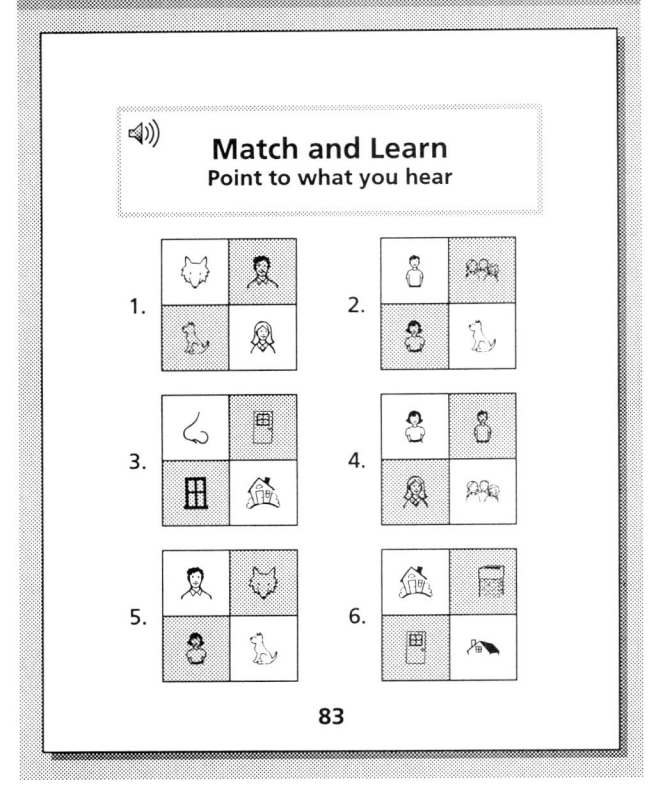

Now look at frame 4. Point to the *puer*. Did you point to the boy? Good job. Now point to the *liberi*. Did you point to the group of children? Well done. Now point to the *femina*. You should have pointed to the woman. Now last of all, point to the *puella*. Did you choose the girl? That's right.

Now look at frame 5. Point to the *canis*. You should have pointed to the dog. Now point to the *puella*. You should have pointed to the girl. Now point to the *vir*. Did you point to the man? That's right! Now point to the *lupus*. The *lupus* is the wolf, right?

Now look at frame 6. Point to the *domus*. The *domus* is the house. Now point to the *caminus*. Can you guess which one that is? Yes, it's the chimney. And what comes out of a

Continued from Children's Activity Book, page 83

caminus? Why, *fumus* of course! Smoke comes out of a *caminus*! Now point to the *janua*. Did you choose the door? Right on. Now last of all, point to the roof. Roof in Latin is *tectum*. Say it out loud: *tectum*. Well done.

Match and Learn

This exercise uses match and learn frames to introduce some more new words that will be used in the story.

Instructions for This Page

Have your children look at the frames in their activity book and point to the pictures as the tape directs them.

Audio Transcript

Narrator: Here are just a few more new words you'll hear in the story. Look at the frames in your activity book and point to what you hear.

Look at frame 1. Point to the *malum*. Did you pick the apple? Right! Now point to the *domus*. Did you choose the house? Good. Now point to the *nasus*. The *nasus* is the nose, of course! Now, last of all, point to the *oculi*. Did you point to the eyes? Right! *Oculi* Is the Latin word for eyes!

Now look at frame 2. Point to the *caminus*. The *caminus* is the chimney. Now point to the *cauda*. Did you choose the tail? In Latin the word for tail is *cauda*. Now point to the *fenestra*. Did you choose the window? Right on. Now point to the *tectum*. It's the roof, right?

Now look at frame 3. Point to the *canis*. The *canis* is the dog, right? Now point to the *arbor*. *Arbor* is the Latin word for tree. Did you point to the tree? Good. Now point to the group of trees, the *silva*. *Silva* is Latin for forest. Say it out loud: *silva*. A *silva* is made up of more than one *arbor*, right? Now, last of all, point to the *janua*. The *janua* is the door.

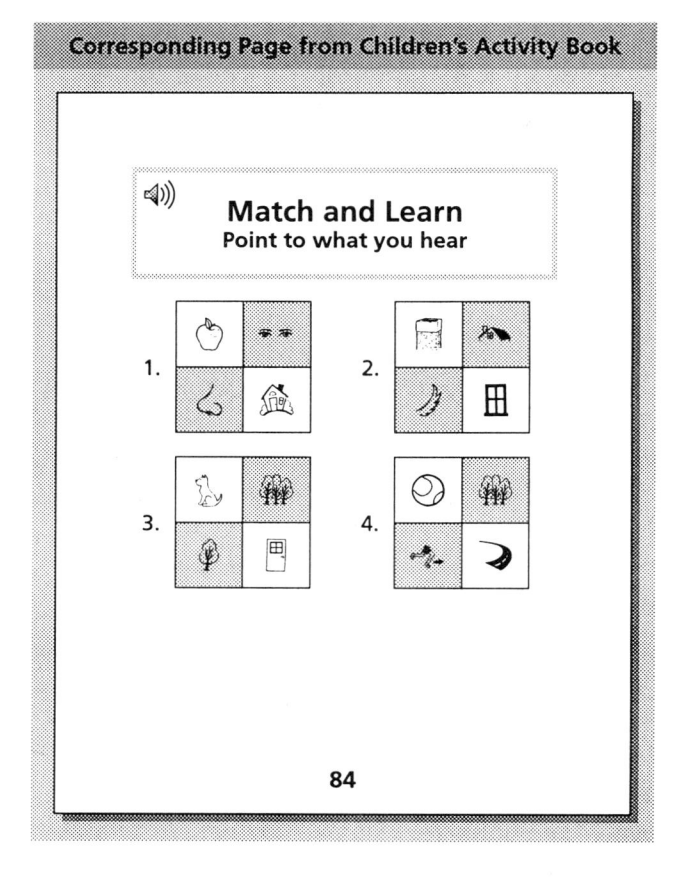

Now look at frame 4. Point to the *silva*. Did you pick the forest? Good! Now point to the *via*. The *via* is the road. *Via* means "road" in Latin. Now point to "runs." *Currit* is the Latin word for "runs." Finally, point to the *pila*. The *pila* is the ball, right? Good memory!

Diglot Weave

The following is the complete diglot-weave story of "The Broken Window," taken from the adult Power-Glide Latin course. As your children listen to the story, they will encounter the new Latin words they have just learned, as well as other simple words and some words they have learned in previous activities. The story format introduces the words in a fun and memorable way, and also lets your children see the actual Latin words on the page and to begin developing their reading ability.

Instructions for This Page

Have your children follow the words of the story in their activity book as they are read on the tape. Here again, as in "The Hungry Giant," English words that are not necessary—because the Latin words include their meaning—are in small, plain font.

Audio Transcript

Narrator: Now listen as I tell the story, the *fabula*, "The Broken Window."

Here is a *pictura* that I drew. *In* the *picturā* you see a *viam*. On one side of this *viae est* a *domus* with a *janua*...a front *janua, et* on the second story, *duae* windows, *duae fenestrae*. If you could look into the *fenestram* on the right, you would *videre* a man, a *virum* sitting at the *fenestram*. No doubt the *vir est* the owner, the *dominus* of the house.

Corresponding Page from Children's Activity Book

Diglot Weave
The Broken Window

Here is a *pictura* that I drew. *In* the *picturā* you see a *viam*. On one side of this *viae est* a *domus* with a *janua*...a front *janua, et* on the second story, *duae* windows, *duae fenestrae*. If you could look into the *fenestram* on the right, you would *videre* a man, a *virum* sitting at the *fenestram*. No doubt the *vir est* the owner, the *dominus* of the house.

85

Diglot Weave

This is the next page of the diglot-weave story of "The Broken Window."

Instructions for This Page

Have your children follow the words of the story in their activity book as they are read on the tape.

Audio Transcript

Narrator: He sits there *apud* the *fenestram, silente* reading a *librum. In* the air in front of the *domum*, there is a small *objectum*, a small round *pila*. Do you see the *pilam?* Although you don't see them, there are four children (*liberi*) in the story: *duo* boys (*pueri*) *et duae* girls (*puellae*). The *liberi* are playing (*ludunt*) with the *pilā*. On this *latere* of the *viae* there is a woods...a *silva*.

Corresponding Page from Children's Activity Book

He sits there *apud* the *fenestram, silente* reading a *librum. In* the air in front of the *domum*, there is a small *objectum*, a small round *pila*. Do you see the *pilam?* Although you don't see them, there are four children (*liberi*) in the story: *duo* boys (*pueri*) *et duae* girls (*puellae*). The *liberi* are playing (*ludunt*) with the *pilā*. On this *latere* of the *viae* there is a woods...a *silva*.

86

Diglot Weave

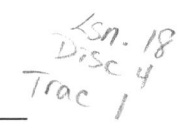

This is the next page of the diglot-weave story of "The Broken Window."

Instructions for This Page

Have your children follow the words of the story in their activity book as they are read on the tape.

Audio Transcript

Narrator: As you well know, a *silva*, where there are *multae arbores*, can be a very dangerous *locus*. In the *silvā* there might be wild *bestiae*, for example, maybe a big, bad *lupus* or a grizzly *ursus*. Such wild *bestiae* are not *amici* of children. Wild *bestiae sunt* dangerous, <u>very</u> *periculosae*. They have been known to attack *liberos* and carry them off. That is very frightening, isn't it?

Corresponding Page from Children's Activity Book

As you well know, a *silva*, where there are *multae arbores*, can be a very dangerous *locus*.

In the *silvā* there might be wild *bestiae*, for example, maybe a big, bad *lupus* or a grizzly *ursus*. Such wild *bestiae* are not *amici* of children. Wild *bestiae sunt* dangerous, <u>very</u> *periculosae*. They have been known to attack *liberos* and carry them off. That is very frightening, isn't it?

Diglot Weave

This is the next page of the diglot-weave story of "The Broken Window."

Instructions for This Page

Have your children follow the words of the story in their activity book as they are read on the tape.

Audio Transcript

Narrator: Now notice this: something is sticking out from behind one of the *arboris* there in the *silvā*. Do you see it? There is an arrow, a *sagitta,* pointing to it. What could the *sagitta* be pointing to? Could it be the *cauda* of a wild *bestiae?* Could it be the *cauda* of a big, bad *lupi?* If it is, then there *est* grave danger...*grave periculum*...lurking behind the *arborem*.

Corresponding Page from Children's Activity Book

Now notice this: something is sticking out from behind one of the *arboris* there in the *silvā*. Do you see it? There is an arrow, a *sagitta,* pointing to it. What could the *sagitta* be pointing to? Could it be the *cauda* of a wild *bestiae?* Could it be the *cauda* of a big, bad *lupi?* If it is, then there *est* grave danger...*grave periculum*...lurking behind the *arborem*.

88

Power-Glide **Children's Latin**

Diglot Weave

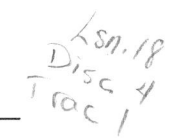

This is the next page of the diglot-weave story of "The Broken Window."

Instructions for This Page

Have your children follow the words of the story in their activity book as they are read on the tape.

Audio Transcript

🔊 Narrator: But the *liberi* don't think about the *periculo*. There's no warning sign that says PERICULUM, keep out! The *liberi* feel safe. They don't sense any *periculum*.

Look at the *picturam* again. Look at the *domum*. Besides the *januam* and *fenestras*, the *domus* has a *tectum* on top (like every *domus* has) and, sticking up out of the *tecto* is a *caminus*. Billowing out of the *camino est fumus*.

Corresponding Page from Children's Activity Book

But the *liberi* don't think about the *periculo*. There's no warning sign that says PERICULUM, keep out! The *liberi* feel safe. They don't sense any *periculum*.

Look at the *picturam* again. Look at the *domum*. Besides the *januam* and *fenestras*, the *domus* has a *tectum* on top (like every *domus* has) and, sticking up out of the *tecto* is a *caminus*. Billowing out of the *camino est fumus*.

89

Diglot Weave

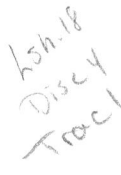

This is the next page of the diglot-weave story of "The Broken Window."

Instructions for This Page

Have your children follow the words of the story in their activity book as they are read on the tape.

Audio Transcript

Narrator: In the *picturā*, besides the *silvam*, the *viam*, the *liberos* and the *domum*, there is a fruit *arbor* on one *latere* of the *domus*, and hanging from a limb of the *arbore est unum malum*. You don't see her in the *picturā*, but there is a *femina*, walking down the *viam*. No doubt her *oculi* have seen the *liberos*, playing with the *pilā* in the *viā*.

Corresponding Page from Children's Activity Book

In the *picturā*, besides the *silvam*, the *viam*, the *liberos* and the *domum*, there is a fruit *arbor* on one *latere* of the *domus*, and hanging from a limb of the *arbore est unum malum*. You don't see her in the *picturā*, but there is a *femina*, walking down the *viam*. No doubt her *oculi* have seen the *liberos*, playing with the *pilā* in the *viā*.

Power-Glide **Children's Latin**

Diglot Weave

This is the next page of the diglot-weave story of "The Broken Window."

Instructions for This Page

Have your children follow the words of the story in their activity book as they are read on the tape.

Audio Transcript

Narrator: You have probably already guessed what happens. A *puer* throws the *pilam*, and it flies high in the air. Do you suppose that the *pila* crashes through the *januam*? No, it doesn't crash through the *januam*. Do you suppose the *pila* lands on the *tecto*? No, it doesn't land on the *tecto*. Do you suppose that it goes down the *camino*? No, it *non* goes down the *camino*.

Corresponding Page from Children's Activity Book

You have probably already guessed what happens. A *puer* throws the *pilam*, and it flies high in the air. Do you suppose that the *pila* crashes through the *januam*? No, it doesn't crash through the *januam*. Do you suppose the *pila* lands on the *tecto*? No, it doesn't land on the *tecto*. Do you suppose that it goes down the *camino*? No, it *non* goes down the *camino*.

The Broken Window — Diglot Weave

Diglot Weave

This is the next page of the diglot-weave story of "The Broken Window."

Instructions for This Page

Have your children follow the words of the story in their activity book as they are read on the tape.

Audio Transcript

Narrator: Do you suppose that it crashes into the apple *arborem* and knocks that last *malum* to the *terram*? No, it *non* crashes into the apple *arborem*. Do you suppose that it crashes through the *fenestram* where the *vir* is sitting, *silente* reading a *librum*? You're right, that's what happens: the *pila* crashes through the *fenestram* and hits the *virum* right in his *nasu*. Ouch!

Corresponding Page from Children's Activity Book

Do you suppose that it crashes into the apple *arborem* and knocks that last *malum* to the *terram*? No, it *non* crashes into the apple *arborem*. Do you suppose that it crashes through the *fenestram* where the *vir* is sitting, *silente* reading a *librum*? You're right, that's what happens: the *pila* crashes through the *fenestram* and hits the *virum* right in his *nasu*. Ouch!

92

Power-Glide **Children's Latin**

Diglot Weave

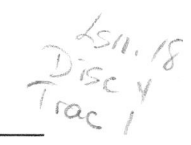

This is the next page of the diglot-weave story of "The Broken Window."

Instructions for This Page

Have your children follow the words of the story in their activity book as they are read on the tape.

Audio Transcript

Narrator: Now what do you think will happen? What do you think the *liberi* will do? Do you suppose the *liberi* walk up *ad* the *domum* and *pulsant* on the *januā* and offer to pay for repair of the *fenestrae?* Or do you suppose the naughty *liberi currunt* as fast as they can into the *silvam?* In a *momento* you'll find out.

Corresponding Page from Children's Activity Book

Now what do you think will happen? What do you think the *liberi* will do? Do you suppose the *liberi* walk up *ad* the *domum* and *pulsant* on the *januā* and offer to pay for repair of the *fenestrae?* Or do you suppose the naughty *liberi currunt* as fast as they can into the *silvam?* In a *momento* you'll find out.

93

The Broken Window   Diglot Weave

Diglot Weave

This is the next page of the diglot-weave story of "The Broken Window."

Instructions for This Page

Have your children follow the words of the story in their activity book as they are read on the tape.

Audio Transcript

Narrator: When the *pila* breaks the *fenestram* and smacks the *virum* in his *naso*, he jumps up. He is *iratus*, very *iratus*...*furiosus*. Why *est* the *vir iratus*? Well, wouldn't you be *iratus* if someone hit a *pilam* through the *fenestram* of your *domus* and it smacked you right in the *naso*? Of course you would be *iratus*, you would be *valde iratus*, *furiosus*. And so is this *vir*. Looking out the *fenestrā* he sees the *liberos* running away.

Corresponding Page from Children's Activity Book

When the *pila* breaks the *fenestram* and smacks the *virum* in his *naso*, he jumps up. He is *iratus*, very *iratus*...*furiosus*. Why *est* the *vir iratus*? Well, wouldn't you be *iratus* if someone hit a *pilam* through the *fenestram* of your *domus* and it smacked you right in the *naso*? Of course you would be *iratus*, you would be *valde iratus*, *furiosus*. And so is this *vir*. Looking out the *fenestrā* he sees the *liberos* running away.

94

Diglot Weave

This is the next page of the diglot-weave story of "The Broken Window."

Instructions for This Page

Have your children follow the words of the story in their activity book as they are read on the tape.

Audio Transcript

Narrator: They *currunt* as fast as they can up the *viam*, toward the *feminam*. Do you think her sharp *oculi* saw what happened? Of course they *viderunt*, and the *femina exclamat: Liberi,* stop! And the *vir in* the *domi exclamat: Liberi,* stop! But the *liberi non* stop. They *currunt* as fast as they *possunt* into the *silvam*. Naughty *liberi!*

Corresponding Page from Children's Activity Book

They *currunt* as fast as they can up the *viam*, toward the *feminam*. Do you think her sharp *oculi* saw what happened? Of course they *viderunt*, and the *femina exclamat: Liberi,* stop! And the *vir in* the *domi exclamat: Liberi,* stop! But the *liberi non* stop. They *currunt* as fast as they *possunt* into the *silvam*. Naughty *liberi!*

95

Diglot Weave

This is the next page of the diglot-weave story of "The Broken Window."

Instructions for This Page

Have your children follow the words of the story in their activity book as they are read on the tape.

Audio Transcript

Narrator: Now what do you think the *vir* will do? Will he throw the *pilam* at the *liberos?* Will he climb up the *camino* onto the *tectum* and jump off? Will he jump out the *fenestrā et* climb the *arborem et* pick the *malum et* eat it? Nonsense!

As you already know, the *liberi* flee into the *silvam*. They are afraid of the *virum*. They fear that the *vir* will catch them *et* punish them. What punishment, what *punitionem,* do you think they fear?

Corresponding Page from Children's Activity Book

Now what do you think the *vir* will do? Will he throw the *pilam* at the *liberos?* Will he climb up the *camino* onto the *tectum* and jump off? Will he jump out the *fenestrā et* climb the *arborem et* pick the *malum et* eat it? Nonsense!

As you already know, the *liberi* flee into the *silvam*. They are afraid of the *virum*. They fear that the *vir* will catch them *et* punish them. What punishment, what *punitionem,* do you think they fear?

Power-Glide **Children's Latin**

Diglot Weave

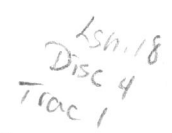

This is the next page of the diglot-weave story of "The Broken Window."

Instructions for This Page

Have your children follow the words of the story in their activity book as they are read on the tape.

Audio Transcript

Narrator: They fear they'll have to pay for the shattered *fenestrae*. Do you think they deserve *punitionem*? Should they have to pay for the broken *fenestrae*? Does the *vir* have the right to make them pay for the repair of the broken *fenestrae*…and maybe for a broken *naso* as well?

Corresponding Page from Children's Activity Book

They fear they'll have to pay for the shattered *fenestrae*. Do you think they deserve *punitionem*? Should they have to pay for the broken *fenestrae*? Does the *vir* have the right to make them pay for the repair of the broken *fenestrae*…and maybe for a broken *naso* as well?

97

The Broken Window   Diglot Weave

Diglot Weave

This is the next page of the diglot-weave story of "The Broken Window."

Instructions for This Page

Have your children follow the words of the story in their activity book as they are read on the tape.

Audio Transcript

Narrator: Now look at the *silvam* in the *picturā* again. That tiny *objectum* you can see in the *silvā*, behind the *arborem*, could it be the bushy *cauda* of a big, bad *lupi*? Perhaps he *silente* crouches there, waiting to pounce on the unsuspecting *liberos*. Listen now to the *continuationem* of the *fabulae*.

Corresponding Page from Children's Activity Book

Now look at the *silvam* in the *picturā* again. That tiny *objectum* you can see in the *silvā*, behind the *arborem*, could it be the bushy *cauda* of a big, bad *lupi*? Perhaps he *silente* crouches there, waiting to pounce on the unsuspecting *liberos*. Listen now to the *continuationem* of the *fabulae*.

98

Power-Glide **Children's Latin**

Diglot Weave

This is the next page of the diglot-weave story of "The Broken Window."

Instructions for This Page

Have your children follow the words of the story in their activity book as they are read on the tape.

Audio Transcript

🔊 Narrator: It *is* the big, bad *lupus*. And he's so *esuriens* that his stomach is growling. Just as the big, bad *lupus* moves menacingly toward them, the *liberi* see *Sagittam*, the St. Bernard *canis* that likes to play in the *silvā* with the *liberis*. "*Sagitta, Sagitta,*" they *exclamant*. *Sagitta* comes *currens*, chases the fleeing *lupum*, bites him on his bushy *caudam* and saves the *liberos*.

Corresponding Page from Children's Activity Book

It *is* the big, bad *lupus*. And he's so *esuriens* that his stomach is growling. Just as the big, bad *lupus* moves menacingly toward them, the *liberi* see *Sagittam*, the St. Bernard *canis* that likes to play in the *silvā* with the *liberis*. "*Sagitta, Sagitta,*" they *exclamant*. *Sagitta* comes *currens*, chases the fleeing *lupum*, bites him on his bushy *caudam* and saves the *liberos*.

99

Diglot Weave

This is the next page of the diglot-weave story of "The Broken Window."

Instructions for This Page

Have your children follow the words of the story in their activity book as they are read on the tape.

Audio Transcript

Narrator: Now the *liberi* feel sorry that they *currerunt* away. They go back to the *domum*, *pulsant* on the *januā*, *et* offer to pay for the shattered *fenestrā* and any other damage they *fecerunt*. Now the *vir* is no longer *furiosus*. He saw what happened. He *dicit* to the *liberis*. "That's okay. The shattered *fenestra* doesn't matter, and my *nasus* will heal. I'm just glad the big bad *lupus* didn't get you."

Corresponding Page from Children's Activity Book

Now the *liberi* feel sorry that they *currerunt* away. They go back to the *domum*, *pulsant* on the *januā*, *et* offer to pay for the shattered *fenestrā* and any other damage they *fecerunt*. Now the *vir* is no longer *furiosus*. He saw what happened. He *dicit* to the *liberis*. "That's okay. The shattered *fenestra* doesn't matter, and my *nasus* will heal. I'm just glad the big bad *lupus* didn't get you."

Power-Glide **Children's Latin**

Diglot Weave

This is the next page of the diglot-weave story of "The Broken Window."

Instructions for This Page

Have your children follow the words of the story in their activity book as they are read on the tape.

Audio Transcript

Narrator: What a nice *vir!* And what a happy *finis* to what could have ended up a real *tragaedia*.

Corresponding Page from Children's Activity Book

What a nice *vir!* And what a happy *finis* to what could have ended up a real *tragaedia*.

101

The Broken Window | Diglot Weave

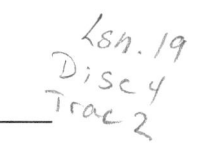

Up and Up, to Antonia's

This section contains an audio transcript of the adventure story your children will hear on the tape.

Instructions for This Page

Have your children listen carefully as the adventure story is read on the tape. Encourage your children to take an active part in listening to the adventure story. Ask them to respond to things they hear and have them say out loud words said by the characters on the tape.

Younger children might enjoy coloring the picture as the adventure story is read. Older children may want to follow along with the written audio transcript provided in this *Parent's Guide*.

Audio Transcript

Narrator 2: The Adventure Continues: Up and Up, to Antonia's!

Narrator: As Aeneas finishes the story of "The Broken Window" you look around and realize that the fire has died down and night has fallen. You yawn long but quietly and then say, "Thanks for telling us that story, Aeneas. I liked it!"

Aeneas: I'm glad. And now it's time for sleep. I'll wake you early in the morning. Good night! Or as we say in Latin, *bonam noctem!*

Henry: I don't think I could stay awake much longer, even if I wanted to. *Bonam noctem,* everyone!

Jill: *Bonam noctem!*

Narrator: You sleep deeply and it hardly seems like any time has passed when Aeneas gently shakes you in the morning. He wakes Jill and Henry as well, and after a quick breakfast, you are on your way again. Mist from the waterfall just behind you fills the jungle, hanging thickly over plants and around tree trunks until the hot tropical sun burns it away. Now the trail through the jungle is lighter than before, because the trees don't grow so thick and close together this high up. Also, the leaves are not so brilliant green. The sounds are a bit different here too, and Aeneas tells you about the creatures that live in these high jungles as you go along.

Late that afternoon, after winding your way all day through the jungle, climbing ever higher and higher into the mountains, Aeneas stops to let you rest.

Aeneas: Let's rest here for a few minutes. You are all good hikers, but you must be getting tired by now. Your young legs have taken you many miles today, and the pass that you seek is only a few hours away now. However, I think we must soon stop for the night—at the

Continued from Children's Activity Book, page 103

home of my old friend Antonia, as I told you before.

Jill: Where does she live, Aeneas? I haven't seen any houses since we came up the cliffs by the waterfall.

Henry: Yeah. It's hard to imagine anyone living in such a remote place. Doesn't she like to be by other people?

Aeneas: Her home is very near here. And actually, she likes the company of others very much. You see, although her home is far from where most of the people on our side of the island live, I think that you would have a hard time finding many of our people who have not visited Antonia at least once or twice. She is a very wise and kind woman, and many people come to her for help in hard times, to get advice and to find peace from the cares of life for awhile.

Narrator: "She sounds like a really nice person to visit, Aeneas," you say.

Aeneas: She is indeed a wonderful friend to everyone. Come, let's finish our journey to her home. It's just a bit further now.

Narrator: As the sun sets behind you and the jungle around you slowly fills with shadows, you hike on toward Antonia's house. At last, when you think you can hardly bring yourself to put one foot in front of the other, you see a light ahead.

Aeneas: Ah! Here we are, my friends! And there is Antonia, still working by lantern light at the big weaving loom on her front porch.

Jill: Wow, I've never seen a real loom before. It looks like she's making a blanket or something. Look, she has seen us coming!

Aeneas: *Salve*, Antonia!

Antonia: *Salve*, Aeneas! It is you, isn't it? My, it's been such a long time. But who are your friends?

Aeneas: They are children from the other side of the island. I am leading them through the high pass so they can rejoin their friends. They are learning Latin while they are here with us.

Antonia: Ah! Wonderful! *Loqueris latine?*

Jill: Yes, a little. It's really fun to learn.

Henry: Yeah.

Antonia: I'm glad you like it. Latin is such a valuable and beautiful language. Now then, come inside and be comfortable, and have something to eat.

Narrator: "Thank you, Antonia," you say. And you all go inside together. After supper, you go back out on the large front porch to enjoy the cool evening air and the sounds of the jungle at night. You look carefully at Antonia's loom.

Jill: This loom is really neat, Antonia. Is it hard to weave things?

Antonia: No, it's not hard, Jill. It just takes years of practice. In that way, it's kind of like learning to speak another language: It isn't difficult, but you do need to practice it often in order to really learn to understand and speak well. Practice is the key!

Henry: Practice, huh? That makes four things to remember. Marcus told us to build on what we already know and to make learning fun, Aeneas taught us to not stress or to try to learn everything all at once, and now you've said we should practice. Build on what we know, make learning fun, don't stress, and practice. We can do that!

Narrator: "Yeah!" you agree.

Antonia: Wonderful! Now I'll give you a chance to practice your Latin a bit. I'll tell you a very short story, one of my favorites that I learned when I was just a child. You listen carefully and then practice until you can tell it back to me mostly in Latin. You may need to practice for a little while, but if you do, the words you learn will be yours forever. Are you willing to try?

Jill: Yes, of course, Antonia!

Power-Glide **Children's Latin**

Story Telling

This activity introduces the short story of "The Key to the King's Kingdom." It teaches comprehension and word identification skills. Your children will first learn some new words, then follow along as a story is told using those new words, and finally tell the story using the familiar pictures as plot prompts.

Instructions for This Page

Have your children look at the picture in their activity book as the story is introduced.

Audio Transcript

Narrator2: Activity: Story Telling. The Key to the King's Kingdom.

Narrator: The story Antonia tells you is called *Clavis Regno Regis*, "The Key to the King's Kingdom."

Corresponding Page from Children's Activity Book

Story Telling
The Key to the King's Kingdom

104

The Key to the King's Kingdom
Story Telling

Scatter Chart

This exercise uses a Scatter Chart to introduce some new Latin words that will be used in the story of "The Key to the King's Kingdom."

Instructions for This Page

Have your children look the pictures on their activity book pages and point to them as the tape directs. Have them say the Latin words out loud as the tape directs.

Audio Transcript

Narrator: Before I tell you this story, lets learn a few of the words you'll hear. Look at the pictures on your activity book page and point to what you hear.

Point to the *rex*. A *rex* is a king. Say it out loud: *rex*. Now point to the *oppidum*. An *oppidum* is a city. Say it out loud: *oppidum*. Now point to the key. "Key" in Latin is *clavis*. Say *clavis* out loud: *clavis*. Now point to the *amphora*. Did you point to the vase? Good. Say it out loud: *amphora*. An *amphora* is a vase. Now point to the *hortus*, the garden. *Hortus* is the Latin word for garden. Say it out loud: *hortus*. Now point to the *mensa in cubiculo*. Did you point to the table in the bedroom? Good! That is the *mensa in cubiculo*! Say *mensa in cubiculo* out loud: *mensa in cubiculo*. Now, last of all, point to the rose, the *rosa*. *Rosa* is a Latin word for a rose. Say it out loud: *rosa*. Good job!

Power-Glide **Children's Latin**

Follow Along

This is the story of "The Key to the King's Kingdom." In your children's activity books only the Latin words appear, but both the Latin and English are read on the tape, line by line. The entire story is understandable because translations are given.

Instructions for This Page

Have your children follow along line by line and picture by picture as the story is read on the tape.

Since the next exercise asks your children to tell this story on their own, using only the pictures, it is important that they learn the story and the words in it well before going on. You may want to have them listen to the entire story two or three times in order to help them become quite familiar with it.

Audio Transcript

Narrator: Now here is the story Antonia tells you. Listen carefully and follow along line by line, looking at the pictures that go along with the story. Remember, after you hear the story it will be your turn to tell it, so pay close attention.

Here you see a king.
Hic vides regem.

Here you see his kingdom.
Hic vides regnum ejus.

And here you see a key.
Et hic vides clavem.

The key to the kingdom it is!
Clavis regno est ea!

In this kingdom there's a town.
In hoc regno est oppidum.

Corresponding Page from Children's Activity Book

Follow Along
Point to what you hear

Clavis Regno Regis!
Hic vides regem.
Hic vides regnum ejus.
Et hic vides clavem.
Clavis regno est ea!

In hoc regno est oppidum.
In oppido est hortus.
In horto est domus.
In domo est cubiculum.
In cubiculo est mensa.
In mensā stat amphora.
In amphorā est rosa.

Rosa in amphorā,
Amphora in mensā,
Mensa in cubiculo,
Cubiculum in domo,
Domus apud hortum,
Hortus in oppido,
Oppidum in regno,
Et haec est illa clavis,
    clavis regis regno.
Uau!

106

In the town there's a garden.
In oppido est hortus.

In the garden there's a house.
In horto est domus.

In the house there's a bedroom.
In domo est cubiculum.

In the bedroom there's a table.
In cubiculo est mensa.

On the table stands a vase.
In mensā stat amphora.

In the vase there's a rose.
In amphorā est rosa.

A rose in a vase,
Rosa in amphorā,

The vase on a table,
Amphora in mensā,

The table in a bedroom,
Mensa in cubiculo,

The Key to the King's Kingdom · P–127 · Follow Along

Continued from Children's Activity Book, page 106

The bedroom in a house,
Cubiculum in domo,

The house by a garden,
Domus apud hortum,

The garden in a town,
Hortus in oppido,

The town in a kingdom,
Oppidum in regno,

And this is that key,
Et haec est illa clavis,

The key to the king's kingdom.
Clavis regis regno.

Wow!

Uau!

Now again, Latin only.
Hic vides regem.

Hic vides regnum ejus.

Et hic vides clavem.

Clavis regno est ea!

In hoc regno est oppidum.

In oppido est hortus.

In horto est domus.

In domo est cubiculum.

In cubiculo est mensa.

In mensā stat amphora.

In amphorā est rosa.

Rosa in amphorā,

Amphora in mensā,

Mensa in cubiculo,

Cubiculum in domo,

Domus apud hortum,

Hortus in oppido,

Oppidum in regno,

Et haec est illa clavis,

   clavis regis regno.

Uau!

Practice in Latin

This exercise invites your children to re-tell the story of "The Key to the King's Kingdom" using all of the new Latin words they have learned. This effectively tests their knowledge of the new words, and re-enforces the new words in their memory.

Instructions for This Page

Have your children look at the pictures and re-tell the story, using as much Latin as they can.

If your children are not ready to tell the story in Latin on their own, help them the first time through and have them try again, or have them go back and listen to the story a couple more times before trying to tell it again.

Audio Transcript

Narrator: Now, see how much of this story you can tell. Look at the pictures in your activity book to remind you how the story goes. After your first telling, review the story before telling it again, even better. And after that, after further preparation, tell it again, better still.

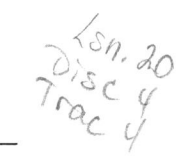

Trek to the High Mountain Pass

This section contains an audio transcript of the adventure story your children will hear on the tape.

Instructions for This Page

Have your children listen carefully as the adventure story is read on the tape. Encourage your children to take an active part in listening to the adventure story. Ask them to respond to things they hear and have them say out loud words the characters say on the tape.

Younger children might enjoy coloring the picture as the adventure story is read. Older children may want to follow along with the written audio transcript provided in this *Parent's Guide*.

Audio Transcript

Narrator 2: The Adventure Continues: Trek to the High Mountain Pass

Narrator: After practicing together for awhile, eventually you, Jill and Henry are each able to tell Antonia's story back to her in Latin.

Antonia: Marvelous, my friends! I am very impressed, and very happy for you. It is wonderful to be young and just discovering all the rich treasures life has to offer. And you three seem determined to learn all you can.

Henry: It's lots of fun to learn new things the way you and Aeneas and Marcus teach them.

Jill: Yeah.

Antonia: I'm glad you're excited about learning. Now, however, perhaps you would like to sleep.

Henry: (yawning) Boy, I sure would. How about you guys?

Narrator: "Uh-ha," you say.

Jill: Me too.

Antonia: Alright then, let's all go inside. I have plenty of room for all of you.

Narrator: Antonia's home is wonderfully comfortable and home-like. You sleep deeply and wake up in the morning refreshed and ready for the final hike to the high mountain pass. You wander out of your room and through the house, and eventually find Aeneas and Antonia already awake and talking to each other on the front porch.

Aeneas: Ah, good morning! You are up early my friend!

Narrator: "Good morning," you reply. "Wow, look at how the mist is hanging over all the trees. It makes everything seem mysterious up here."

Continued from Children's Activity Book, page 109

Antonia: Yes, the world can be a very interesting place, if you take the time to appreciate it.

Henry: Good morning!

Antonia: Ah, good morning Henry! You're up now too, I see.

Henry: Yeah. Jill will probably be out in just a minute too. I heard her moving around in her room when I woke up.

Aeneas: That's good. We should make an early start today. The high mountain pass is very near here, but once we reach it there is still have a good hike ahead of us to get you down to where people live on the other side of the island.

Henry: Oh, yeah. I had forgotten about that.

Aeneas: It's a down hill hike, though, so I'm guessing we'll make good time, once we're through the pass.

Jill: Good morning, everyone!

Aeneas, Antonia, Henry: Good morning, Jill.

Aeneas: Are you ready for the last part of your journey?

Jill: You bet.

Antonia: Good. Now all of you come inside and have some breakfast. Aeneas and I have it all prepared, we were just waiting for you children to wake up.

Henry: Mmmm… I can smell it. It smells wonderful!

Antonia: Good! Now come in and enjoy it.

Narrator: You eat a delicious breakfast and thank Antonia for the food and for letting you stay with her. Then, as the sun rises brilliantly above you, you, Jill, Henry and Aeneas all start out on the last leg of your trek to the high mountain pass that leads to the other side of the island. Just as Aeneas said, it isn't very far from Antonia's house. Before you have hiked even half an hour you come out of the trees and your path leads up through more rocky terrain. And at last, after an hour and a half of good hiking, you reach the pass.

Henry: Wow, the wind blows really hard up here!

Jill: Yeah. I feel like I should be holding on to something, or the wind might blow me right back down the path!

Aeneas: It is very windy here. Let's sit off to the side and rest and talk for a few minutes. There is still plenty of time to hike down and find your group, and before we do, I want to see just how much Latin you have all learned. I challenge you to show me!

Adventure: Trek to the High Mountain Pass   P–132   Trek to the High Mountain Pass

Aeneas' Challenge

This activity reviews and reinforces much of the course material, using a variety of exercise types.

This first exercise begins reviewing some of the vocabulary learned in this course. It uses the familiar match and learn frames.

Instructions for This Page

Have your children point to the pictures in the various frames as directed by the tape.

Since this activity asks your children to remember words which they may not have seen for some time, it is especially important to encourage them to guess boldly and not worry if they do not remember every word perfectly. Also, you may wish to go back to particular sections and review if your children seem to have a hard time recalling particular words.

Audio Transcript

Narrator 2: Activity: Aeneas' Challenge!

Narrator: For the first part of his language challenge, Aeneas says Latin words you have learned and asks you to point to pictures of what he says. Are you ready for the challenge? All right, here we go! Point to what you hear.

First, look at frame 1 in your activity book. Point to the *vir*. Did you point to the man? Good! Now point to the *femina*. It's the woman, right? Now point to the *pila*. A *pila* is a ball, right? Now, last of all, point to the *saxum*. The *saxum* is the rock, right?

Now look at frame 2. Point to the box with *unum quadratum, unus circulus et duo triangula*. It's the bottom white box, right? Now point to the box with *unus circulus, duo quadrata, et una linea*. It's the top gray box, isn't it? Now point to the box with *duo circuli et duae lineae*. It's the bottom gray box, right? Now, what's in the last box? *Unum quadratum et unus circulus*? That's right!

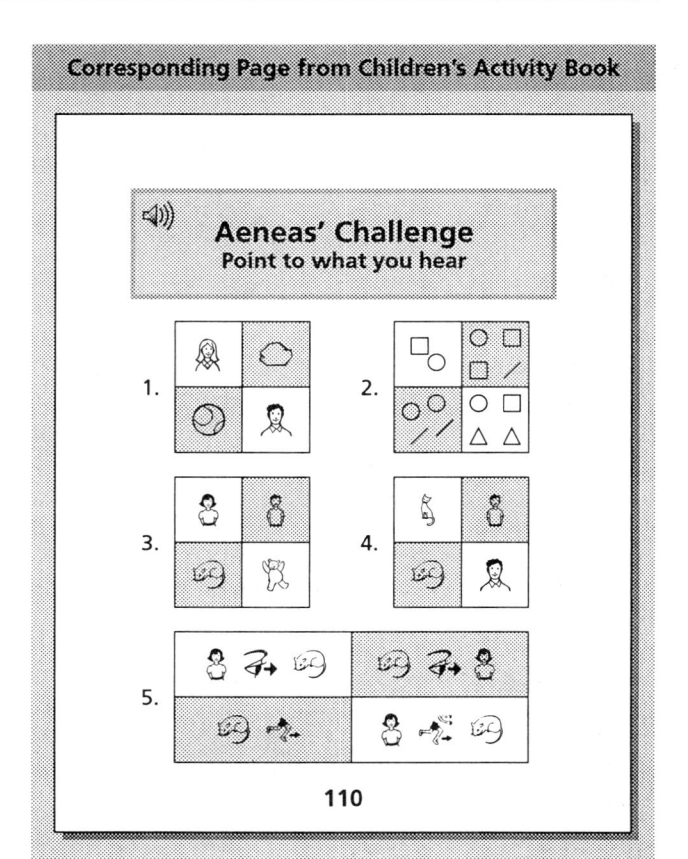

Now look at frame 3. Point to the *puella*. It's the girl, right? Now point to the *puer*. That is the boy, right? Now point to the *mus*. It's the mouse, right? And what's that last picture? That's right—it is an *ursus*, a bear.

Now look at frame 4. Point to the *vir*. It's the man, right? Good. Now point to the *puer*. It's the boy, right? Good. Now point to the *feles*. That's the cat, right? And finally, point to the *mus*. It's the mouse, right? Well done.

Now look at frame 5. Point to *mus currit*. It's the bottom gray box, right? Now point to *mus videt puellam*. It is the top gray box, right? Now point to *puella persequitur murem*. It's the bottom white box, right? Good.

Power-Glide **Children's Latin**

Match and Learn

This exercise continues reviewing some of the vocabulary learned in this course.

Instructions for This Page

Have your children point to the pictures in the various frames as directed by the tape.

Audio Transcript

Look at frame 6. Point to the *serpens*. It is in the top white box, right? Yes. Now point to the *balaena*. Is it in the bottom white box? Yes, it is. Now point to the *arena*. The *arena* is in the bottom gray box, right? Yes. Now point to *cogitavit*. That is in the top white box, right? No, it is in the top gray box.

Now look at frame 7. Point to the thing that is *ruber*. Did you point to the cherries? That's right! Cherries are *ruber* color—red! Now point to the thing that is *flavus*. Did you point to the banana? Well done! The banana is yellow, *flavus* color. Now point to the thing that is *caeruleus*. Did you choose the water? Water is *caeruleus* in the ocean.

Now look at frame 8. Point to the thing that is *purpureus*. Did you point to the grapes? That's right! Grapes are *purpureus* color—they are purple! Now point to the thing that is *luteus*. Did you point to the carrot? Carrots are orange, *luteus* color, aren't they? Now point to the thing that is *roseus*. Did you choose the flower? Good! The flower is *roseus* color—pink!

Now look at frame 9. Point to the *rex*. Did you point to the king? Good! Now point to the *amphora*. It's in the top gray box, right? Now point to the *oppidum*. That's the town, right? Finally, point to the *clavis*. A *clavis* is a key.

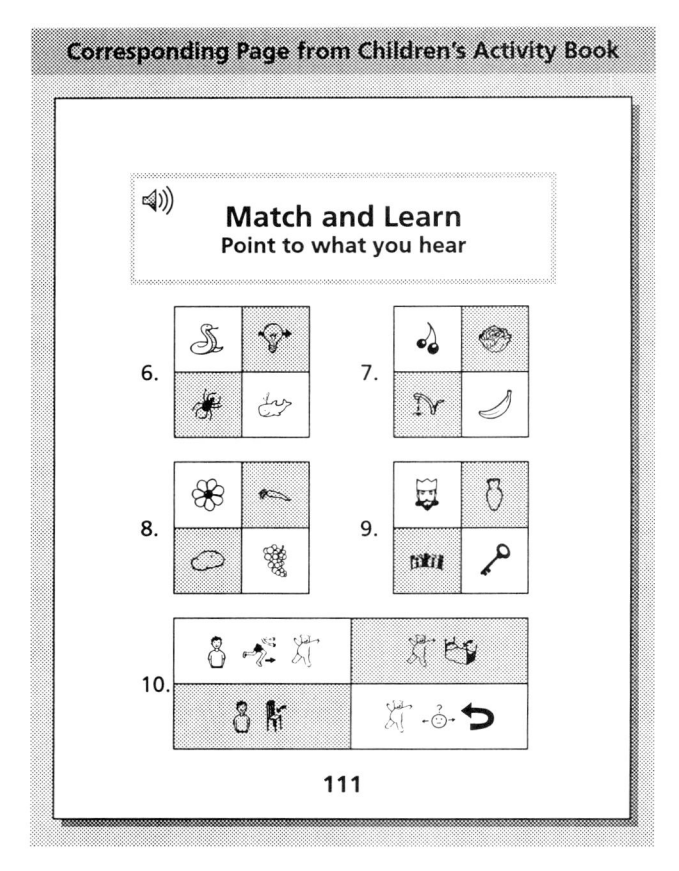

Look at frame 10. Point to *puer insidit in solo*. Did you point to the bottom gray box? Good. Now point to *ursus jacet in solo*. It's is in the top gray box, right? Point to *ursus dubitat, deinde tergum vertit*. This is in the bottom white box, right? Now point to *puer persequitur ursum*. Did you point to the top white box? Good.

Aeneas' Challenge — Match and Learn

Power-Glide **Children's Latin**

Match and Learn

This exercise continues reviewing vocabulary.

Instructions for This Page

Have your children point to the pictures in the various frames as directed by the tape.

Audio Transcript

Narrator: Here are some more frames. See how many of these words you can remember.

Look at frame 11. Point to the *manus*. Did you point to the hand? Good! Now point to the *caput*. Did you point to the head? Good! Finally, point to the *crus*. Did you point to the leg? That's right.

Now look at frame 12. Point to the *crūs*. It's in the top white box, right? Now point to the *pes*. That's the foot, right? Now point to the *ōs*. It's the mouth, right? Finally, point to the *capillī*. It's in the bottom gray box, right? Good.

Now look at frame 13. Point to the *mentum*. Did you point to the chin? Good! Now point to the *oculus*. Did you point to the eye? Good! Finally, point to the *auris*. Did you point to the ear? That's right!

Now look at frame 14. Point to the *domus*. The *domus* is the house, right? Yes. Now point to the *caminus*. Can you guess which one that is? Yes, it's the chimney. And what comes out of a *caminus*? Point to what comes out of a *caminus* and say what it is out loud. Did you point to the *fumus* and say *fumus* out loud? Good!

Now look at frame 15. Point to the *tectum*. That's the roof, isn't it? Now point to the *janua*. That's the door. Now point to the *pila*. Did you point to the ball? Good. Now point to the *nasus*. That's the nose, right? Good.

Now look at frame 16. Point to the *malum*. That's the top gray box, right? Now point to the *lupus*. That's the wolf. Now point to the *cauda*. Did you point to the tail? Good! Now point to the *fenestra*. That's the window, right? Good.

Corresponding Page from Children's Activity Book

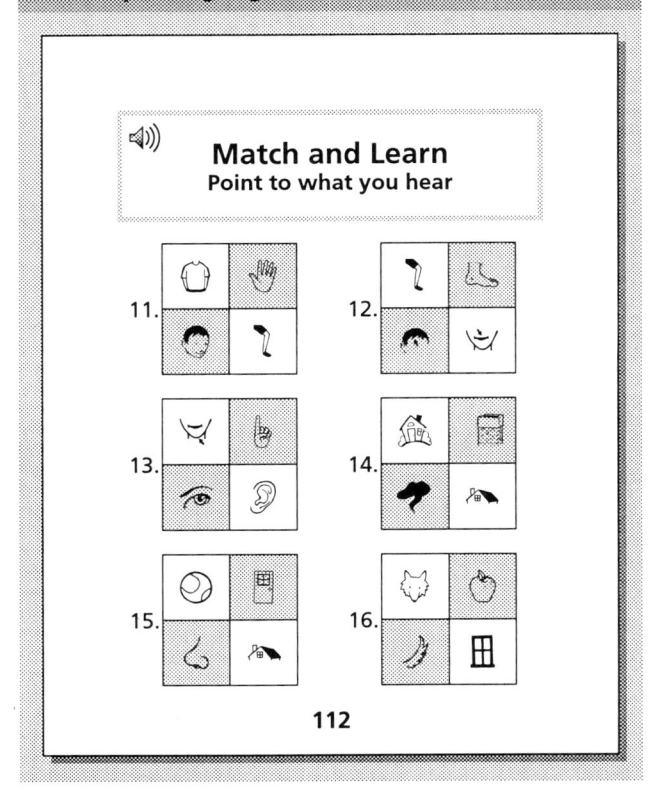

Match and Learn
Point to what you hear

11. 12. 13. 14. 15. 16.

112

Aeneas' Challenge — P–135 — Match and Learn

Match and Learn

This exercise tests your children's memory of the vocabulary just reviewed. In this exercise words from the entire course are mixed together.

Instructions for This Page

Have your children point to the pictures as directed by the tape. Have your children pause the tape as needed to have time to give their answers.

This exercise is more challenging than the previous ones. Encourage your children to do their best and not worry if they don't remember all the words perfectly.

Audio Transcript

Narrator: You did a good job with those matching frames! Once Aeneas has challenged your ability to remember words of the same kind grouped together, he mixes all the words up and challenges you to remember them that way. Let's see if you can! In this activity, I'll simply say the Latin word, followed by the English one.

Look at the frame on your activity book page. Point to the *circulus*. The circle. Now the *bracchium*. The arm. The *saxum*. The rock. The *domus*. The house. The *puella*. The girl. The *lupus*. The wolf. The *femina*. The woman. The *auris*. The ear. The *fumus*. The smoke.

How did you do? Did you remember most of them? Good!

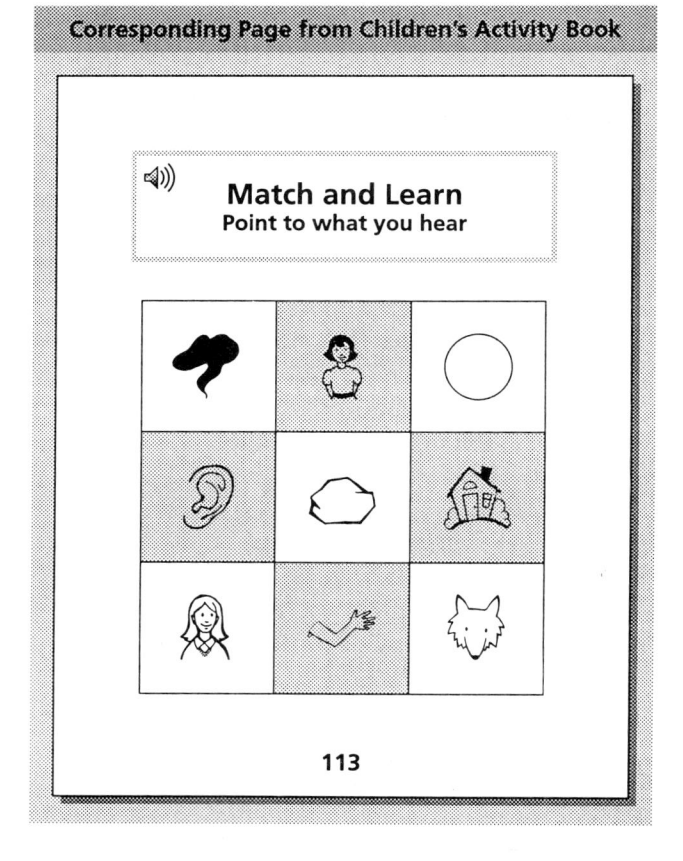

Corresponding Page from Children's Activity Book

Match and Learn
Point to what you hear

113

Power-Glide **Children's Latin**

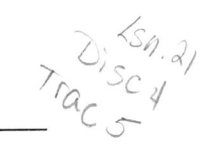

Match and Learn

This exercise tests your children's memory of the vocabulary just reviewed. In this exercise words from the entire course are mixed together.

Instructions for This Page

Have your children point to the pictures as directed by the tape. Have your children pause the tape as needed to have time to give their answers.

Audio Transcript

Narrator: Here is another frame. Point to what you hear.

A *puer*. A boy. An *arbor*. A tree. Something that is *ruber*. The cherries. A *pes*. A foot. A *tectum*. A roof. A *triangulum*. A triangle. A *mus*. A mouse. A *nasus*. A nose. A *linea*. A line.

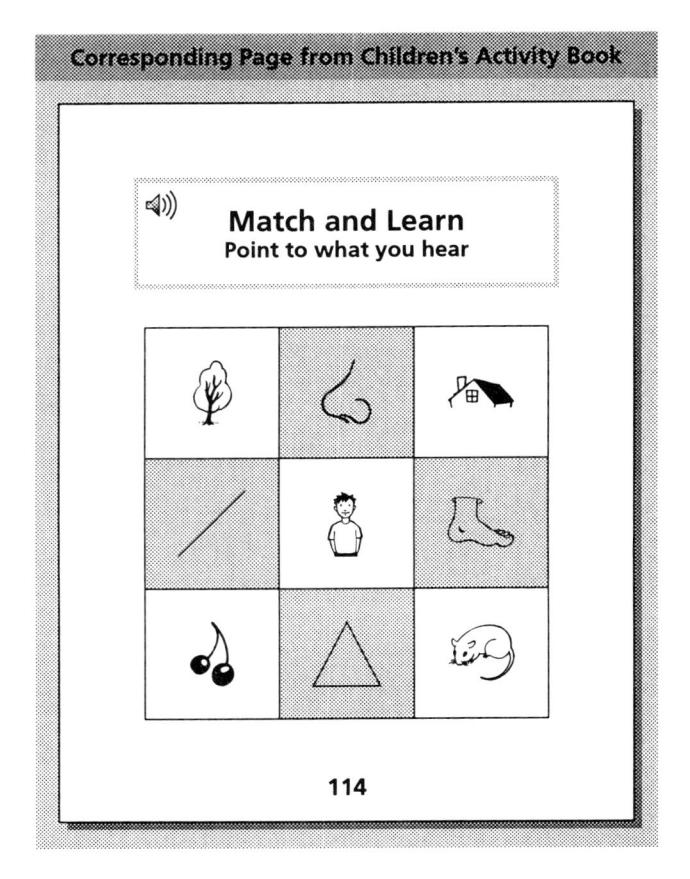

Corresponding Page from Children's Activity Book

Match and Learn
Point to what you hear

114

Aeneas' Challenge   P–137   Match and Learn

Power-Glide **Children's Latin**

Match and Learn

This exercise tests your children's memory of the vocabulary just reviewed. In this exercise words from the entire course are mixed together.

Instructions for This Page

Have your children point to the pictures as directed by the tape. Have your children pause the tape as needed to have time to give their answers.

Audio Transcript

Narrator: Here is one last frame. Point to what you hear.

A *quadratum*. A square. An *oculus*. An eye. An *ursus*. A bear. Something that is *flavus*. The banana. A *canis*. A dog. A *saxum*. A rock. A *pila*. A ball. A *manus*. A hand. A *caput*. A head.

Corresponding Page from Children's Activity Book

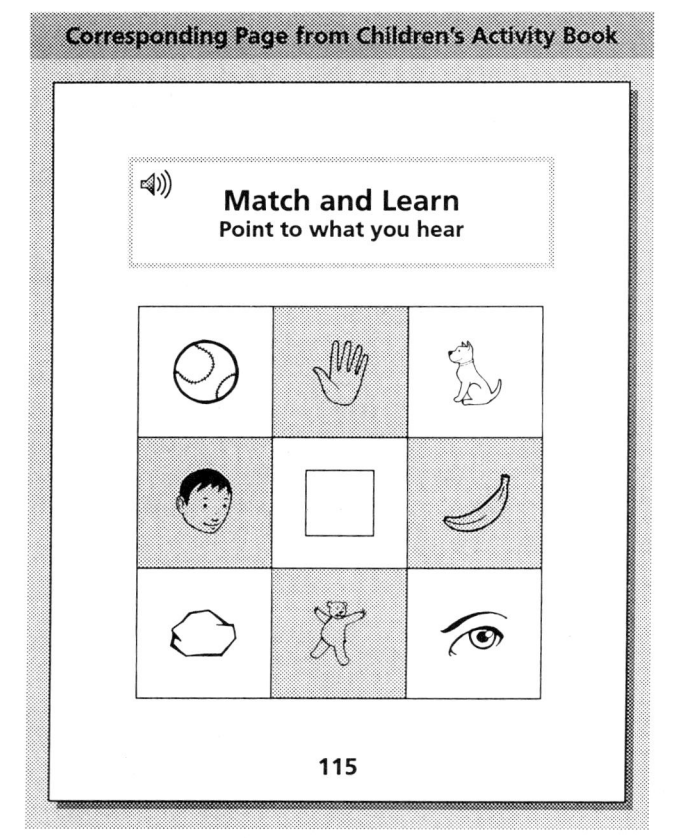

Match and Learn
Point to what you hear

Aeneas' Challenge

Diglot Weave

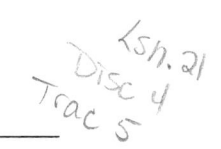

This exercise is a rebus story with Latin words in small print where pictures should be. Your children's task is to put in pictures in the right places.

Instructions for This Page

Have your children find the page of picture stickers at the back of their activity book. Have them look over the pictures before the story begins, so they know what their choices are. The pictures are taken from the "A Hungry Giant" activity and other activities. As the story is told on the tape, have them put the stickers over the small-print Latin words found in circles throughout the story.

Have your children pause the tape as needed to have time to find and put in the right stickers.

Looking at the sticker page, see if your children can guess the picture for the Latin word *ambularet*, meaning 'walked.' They have heard this word earlier, but have not yet been taught a corresponding pictograph for it. If after a while they haven't found *ambularet* on the sticker page, pointed it out to them. The picture for *ambularet* is in the second row and second column from the left (the profile of a person walking).

Audio Transcript

Narrator: After you answer Aeneas' questions, he offers to tell you part of the story, "A Hungry Giant" again, using mostly Latin words. Your challenge is to put in pictures for the Latin words he uses. Look at the story in your activity book. Do you see all the circles with small Latin words written inside them? That is where the pictures go. Take out the stickers included with your course. Look through the them all, then start listening to the story.

Do you have the stickers? Have you looked at all of the pictures? Good! Aeneas began:

One morning before breakfast *pater meus* was taking a walk. While he *ambularet*, he *vidit* a *muscam*. The *musca* was caught in a spider's web. He watched the *arenam* come and eat the *muscam*.

Corresponding Page from Children's Activity Book

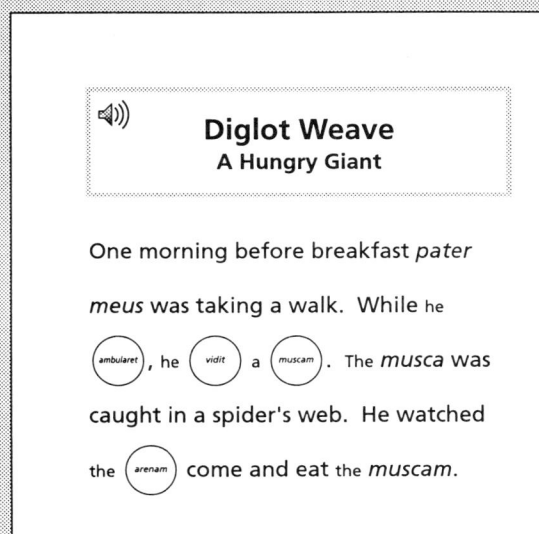

Diglot Weave
A Hungry Giant

One morning before breakfast *pater meus* was taking a walk. While he (ambularet), he (vidit) a (muscam). The *musca* was caught in a spider's web. He watched the (arenam) come and eat the *muscam*.

116

Aeneas' Challenge — P–139 — Diglot Weave

Power-Glide **Children's Latin**

Diglot Weave

This page continues Aeneas' story.

Instructions for This Page

As the story is told on the tape, have your children put the stickers over the small-print Latin words found in circles throughout the story. Have your children pause the tape as needed to have time to find and put in the right stickers.

Audio Transcript

🔊 Narrator: *"Optime!" cogitavit pater meus. "Arena muscam edit. Non placent mihi muscae."*

A moment later, an *avis advenit et arenam edit. "Optime," cogitavit pater meus. "Avis arenam edit. Non placent mihi arenae."*

Corresponding Page from Children's Activity Book

"*Optime!*" (cogitavit) pater meus. "(arena) (muscam) (edit). Non placent mihi muscae."

A moment later, an *avis advenit et arenam edit.* "*Optime,*" *cogitavit pater meus.* "(avis) *arenam edit. Non placent mihi* (arenae)."

117

Aeneas' Challenge · Diglot Weave

Diglot Weave

This page continues Aeneas' story.

Instructions for This Page

As the story is told on the tape, have your children put the stickers over the small-print Latin words found in circles throughout the story. Have your children pause the tape as needed to have time to find and put in the right stickers.

Audio Transcript

Narrator: But after a bit, a *feles venit et avem edit. Et pater meus cogitavit: "Triste est, feles avem edit. Aves placent mihi."*

But after that, a *serpens advenit et felem edit. Et pater meus cogitavit: "Triste est, feles placent mihi."*

Corresponding Page from Children's Activity Book

But after a bit, a (*feles*) venit et avem edit. Et pater meus cogitavit: "Triste est, that the *feles avem edit.* (*avis*) placent mihi."

But after that, a (*serpens*) advenit et felem edit. Et pater meus cogitavit: "Triste est, feles placent mihi."

118

Diglot Weave

This page continues Aeneas' story.

Instructions for This Page

As the story is told on the tape, have your children put the stickers over the small-print Latin words found in circles throughout the story. Have your children pause the tape as needed to have time to find and put in the right stickers.

Audio Transcript

Narrator: But after a bit, *advenit porcus et serpentem edit. Et pater meus cogitavit:* "*Optime, porcus serpentem edit. Non placent mihi serpentes.*"

Before long, *advenit leopardus et porcum edit. Et pater meus cogitavit:*

Corresponding Page from Children's Activity Book

But after a bit, *advenit* (porcus) et *serpentem edit. Et pater meus cogitavit:* "*Optime, porcus serpentem edit. Non placent mihi* (serpentes)."

Before long, *advenit* (leopardus) et (porcum) *edit. Et pater meus cogitavit:*

119

Power-Glide **Children's Latin**

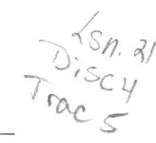

Diglot Weave

This page continues Aeneas' story.

Instructions for This Page

As the story is told on the tape, have your children put the stickers over the small-print Latin words found in circles throughout the story. Have your children pause the tape as needed to have time to find and put in the right stickers.

Audio Transcript

🔊 Narrator: "Wow, *leopardus porcum edit.* Such excitement! – *Talis commotionem!*"

A while later, *advenit crocodilus et leopardum edit. Et pater meus cogitavit:* "Wow, *crocodilus leopardum edit. Talis commotionem! Quid accidet nunc?*"

Corresponding Page from Children's Activity Book

"Wow, *leopardus porcum edit.* Such excitement!—*Talis commotionem!*"

A while later, *advenit* (crocodilus) *et leopardum edit. Et pater meus cogitavit:* "Wow, *crocodilus* (leopardum) *edit. Talis commotionem! Quid accidet nunc?*"

120

Aeneas' Challenge — Diglot Weave

Diglot Weave

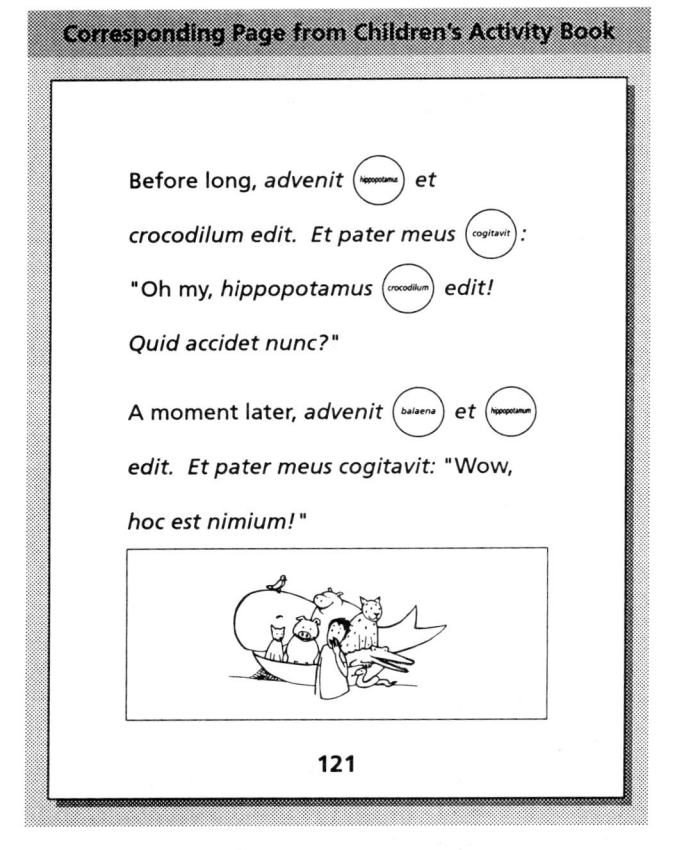

This page continues Aeneas' story.

Instructions for This Page

As the story is told on the tape, have your children put the stickers over the small-print Latin words found in circles throughout the story. Have your children pause the tape as needed to have time to find and put in the right stickers.

Audio Transcript

🔊 Narrator: Before long, *advenit hippopotamus et crocodilum edit. Et pater meus cogitavit:* "Oh my, *hippopotamus crocodilum edit! Quid accidet nunc?*"

A moment later, *advenit balaena et hippopotamum edit. Et pater meus cogitavit:* "Wow, *hoc est nimium!*"

Corresponding Page from Children's Activity Book

Before long, *advenit* (hippopotamus) *et crocodilum edit. Et pater meus* (cogitavit): "Oh my, *hippopotamus* (crocodilum) *edit! Quid accidet nunc?*"

A moment later, *advenit* (balaena) *et* (hippopotamum) *edit. Et pater meus cogitavit:* "Wow, *hoc est nimium!*"

121

Diglot Weave

This page concludes Aeneas' story.

Instructions for This Page

As the story is told on the tape, have your children put the stickers over the small-print Latin words found in circles throughout the story. Have your children pause the tape as needed to have time to find and put in the right stickers.

Audio Transcript

Narrator: Then suddenly a *manus* reached down from the sky *et* picked up *balaenam*. *Pater meus* looked up just as the *gigas* swallowed it whole. *Et cogitavit:* "Wow, this is the first time I've *gigantem vidi*.

Maybe he's still hungry. I'd better get out of here!" And he ran home as fast as he could.

Corresponding Page from Children's Activity Book

Then suddenly a (*manus*) reached down from the sky *et* picked up (*balaenam*). *Pater meus* looked up just as the (*gigas*) swallowed it whole. *Et* he (*cogitavit*): "Wow, this is the first time I've *gigantem* (*vidi*). Maybe he's still hungry. I'd better get out of here. And he (*cucurrit*) home as fast as he could.

122

Aeneas' Challenge — Diglot Weave

Draw and Learn

This exercise invites your children to draw a picture following instructions in Latin.

Instructions for This Page

Have your children listen to the instructions given on the tape and draw what they hear. Although general instructions are given on where to draw each object, there is no "right" way to draw the picture (so long as the right objects are drawn), and no picture key is provided. Once your children have drawn the picture, have them color it and encourage them to show it and other drawings they make to friends, and tell them what the things in the picture are in Latin!

Have your children pause the tape as needed to draw.

Audio Transcript

Narrator: Once you have finished those activities, Aeneas gives you some new challenges. On this chalkboard I'll tell you what to draw, and you draw it, OK? Here we go!

First, near the bottom of your chalkboard in the middle, draw a *domus*. Are you finished? Good.

Now, draw a *via* leading up to the *domus*.

Next, draw an *arbor* next to the *domus*.

And on one side of the *domus*, draw a *puella* with a *feles* by her side.

And on the other side of the *domus*, draw a *mus*, hiding from the *feles*.

Were you able to draw all that? Good work!

Now that it's drawn, it's time to color it.

First, color the sky *caeruleus*.

Next, color the road *niger*.

Next, color the trunk of the *arbor fuscus*, and the top of the *arbor viridis*.

Next, color the walls of the *domus flavus*, and the *tectum ruber*.

Next, color the *feles luteus* and the *mus albus*.

And last of all, color the *puella's* dress or pants *roseus* or *purpureus*, whichever you prefer.

Now you can also show your picture to other people and tell them what the parts and the colors are in Latin!

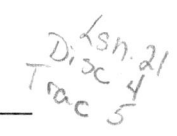

Story Telling

This exercise provides pictures and a plot chain, and invites your children to use the pictures to make up stories of their own.

Instructions for This Page

Have your children remove the Pictograph Cut-out page from the back of their activity books and cut out the pictures along the light gray lines. Once they are all cut up, have them arrange the pictures in order along the blank plot chain on this page in order to create a story. Once the pictures are arranged in order, have your children tell you the story the pictures represent. Then see if they can rearrange the pictures to make another story, and another.

Audio Transcript

Narrator: As the last part of his challenge, Aeneas asks you to tell him stories you make up yourselves using some of the Latin words you have learned. First Jill tells him a story, then Henry, and then it's your turn. Aeneas challenges you to try telling a story using Latin words!

So, go to the back of your activity book and carefully remove the page of cut-out pictures. Use scissors to cut out the individual pictures, then arrange them in the right order on your activity book page to tell a story you make up. Once you have got them all set up in order on your page, tell your story to your mom or dad or your friend, using Latin words for the pictures.

Any story will be fun! And after you've told your first story a few times, and you can tell it very fast and very well, try a different arrangement with other pictures and tell another story. You can make up as many stories as you like. You might even try letting someone else arrange the pictures and you see if you can tell a story using their arrangement

Corresponding Page from Children's Activity Book

Story Telling
Arrange your pictures and tell a story

124

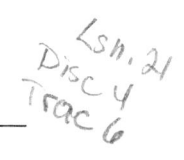

Reunion with Old Friends

This section contains an audio transcript of the adventure story your children will hear on the tape.

Instructions for This Page

Have your children listen carefully as the adventure story is read on the tape.

Encourage your children to take an active part in listening to the adventure story. Ask them to respond to things they hear and have them say out loud words said by the characters on the tape. Younger children might enjoy coloring the picture as the adventure story is read. Older children may want to follow along with the written audio transcript provided in this *Parent's Guide*.

Audio Transcript

Narrator 2: The Adventure Continues: Reunion with Old Friends

Aeneas: Very impressive, my young friends. You have indeed made a good start at learning this marvelous language. I think you now have the tools you need to go on learning Latin at a higher level. Before we conclude our journey together, I'll give you one more hint on how to master a language. It is this: Make learning a lifelong habit.

Jill: Make learning a lifelong habit.

Narrator: "OK," you say. "I think that makes five now: Build on what you already know, Make learning fun, Don't stress, Practice, and Make learning a lifelong habit."

Henry: Good memory!

Aeneas: Yes, good memory indeed. So, like I said, I think you now have the tools you need to continue learning Latin. This is, after all, only the first of many adventures. Power-Glide's adult Latin course contains another adventure that you are now prepared to start on. I hope you will!

Jill: Oh, we will! Don't worry about that, Aeneas. Learning Latin has been the greatest adventure we've ever had. I can hardly wait to learn more!

Henry: Yeah, me too.

Narrator: "And me," you agree.

Aeneas: Excellent, my friends! And now, let's go find your school group.

Narrator: Together you hike down out of the mountains on the English speaking side of the island. You are able to make quick progress, and early in the afternoon you hear voices ahead. It is the other half of your group, just as you had hoped. They are all packed up, and

Continued from Children's Activity Book, page 125

are hiking back down out of the jungle themselves. Aeneas waves goodbye and you run to join your friends, eager to show them how much you have learned. You are on your way home for now, but you're determined to begin another adventure very soon.